Beyond the Tee

Innovative T-Shirt Quilts

9 Extraordinary Designs

Tips for Working with Ties & Other Clothing

*Mary Cannizzaro and
Jen Cannizzaro*

C&T PUBLISHING

Text and photography copyright © 2020 by Mary Cannizzaro and Jen Cannizzaro

Artwork copyright © 2020 by C&T Publishing, Inc.

Publisher: Amy Barrett-Daffin

Creative Director: Gailen Runge

Acquisitions Editor: Roxane Cerda

Managing Editor: Liz Aneloski

Editor: Karla Menaugh

Technical Editor: Debbie Rodgers

Cover/Book Designer: April Mostek

Production Coordinator: Tim Manibusan

Production Editor: Jennifer Warren

Illustrator: Aliza Shalit

Photo Assistant: Gregory Ligman

Photography by Mary Cannizzaro and Jen Cannizzaro, unless otherwise noted

Published by C&T Publishing, Inc., P.O. Box 1456, Lafayette, CA 94549

Library of Congress Cataloging-in-Publication Data

Names: Cannizzaro, Mary, 1947- author. | Cannizzaro, Jen, 1973- author.

Title: Beyond the tee-innovative t-shirt quilts : 9 extraordinary designs, tips for working with ties & other clothing / Mary Cannizzaro and Jen Cannizzaro.

Description: Lafayette, CA : C&T Publishing, [2020]

Identifiers: LCCN 2019056922 | ISBN 9781617459078
ISBN 9781617459085 (ebook)

Subjects: LCSH: Patchwork--Patterns. | Quilting--Patterns. | T-shirts.

Classification: LCC TT835 .C364 2020 | DDC 746.46/041--dc23

LC record available at https://lccn.loc.gov/2019056922

Printed in the USA

10 9 8 7 6 5 4 3 2 1

Dedication

To Roberta Collins, an amazing sister-in-law and aunt, who was our biggest fan. She was the first to like every Facebook post and was always fascinated by every one of our ideas. You are part of this book, Bobbie, and we miss you.

Photo by Meredith Collins

Roberta's sunset

Contents

Projects

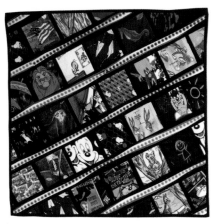

Introduction

A few years ago, a friend asked us to make a quilt from her son's T-shirts. We had made a couple quilts from clothing in the past and had longarm quilted quite a few T-shirt quilts for our clients. We had never been all that excited about working with T-shirts, but this was for someone special. So we agreed to make a quilt for Matthew using the T-shirts he acquired during his four years at East Carolina University.

This first T-shirt quilt was fairly ordinary, with rectangular blocks featuring the motifs from each shirt. We varied the sizes of the rectangles, adding borders to some of them to balance their size. We used different black and white fabrics (our favorites!) for the sashing. Matthew loved his quilt and still thanks us every time he sees us.

We made a few more T-shirt quilts with similar layouts, but we were getting bored. When a family with three children asked us to make quilts from their kids' clothes, we knew it was time to step it up and make quilts that didn't look like they came from T-shirts. We scoured Electric Quilt for blocks with large pieces that could feature a motif. We doodled on paper, incorporating T-shirts into our designs. At one point, one of us said, "You know, we should write a book about making T-shirt quilts that don't look like T-shirt quilts."

Ah … the spoken word. Once it is said, it cannot be taken back. As we continued to work on the quilts for this family, we were unable to shake the idea of writing a book. We began a list of patterns to include and the different skills we had learned that would help others to avoid the mistakes we made. With the help of Diet Coke and venti soy lattes from Starbucks, we put together what we considered a really fun book of ideas and self-published *Beyond the Tee*. In *Beyond the Tee—Innovative T-Shirt Quilts*, we have added new projects, tips, and other information for you. We hope you enjoy the patterns and tips we share!

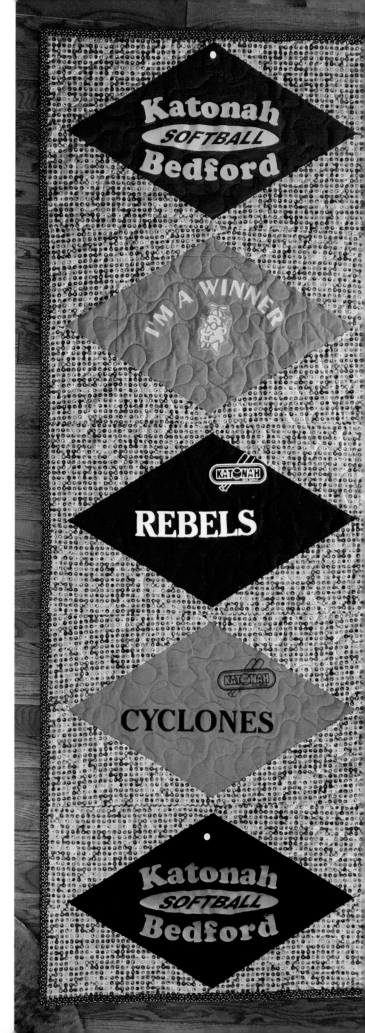

Working with T-Shirts and Clothing

How to Fillet Clothing

T-shirts offer quite a bit of fabric for use in a quilt. When prepared correctly, T-shirts can be cut into different shapes and sizes to accommodate many interesting blocks.

We call the process of cutting up clothing *filleting*. Have you ever filleted a fish? A fish is cut to maximize the amount you cook and eliminate the parts you don't. Filleting a T-shirt works the same way. We cut our clothing with sharp scissors, leaving as much intact as possible. We also save all scraps until the project is finished—you never know when those little pieces will come in handy!

Even the smallest T-shirt has a lot of usable fabric. Cutting it apart in the correct way will give you the most bang for your buck.

Below, we cut the T-shirt up the center back and across the shoulder.

You can also cut up the side seams all the way through the sleeve seam. This gives you two rectangles that are suitable for many designs. If you need the sleeves, cut them off first. Sleeves are a large piece of usable fabric.

Children's pants might look small. But if you remove the elastic from the waistband and cut up the inner leg seam, they offer large sections of fabric for use in your quilt.

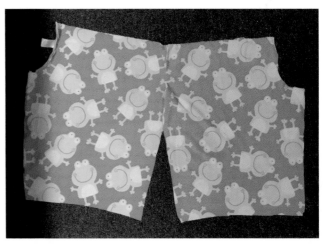

The goal is to maximize the fabric. You may leave some seams intact to allow for larger pieces to work with. Think before you cut!

Make It Work—Solutions to Common Problems

Motif Is Too High

Sometimes, the motif is high up on the front of the shirt. Don't be afraid to use the rib section at the top or add on a piece that you've cut from the side or back of the T-shirt.

The motif is very close to the top edge.

We added a strip from the side above the motif.

Motif Is Too Small

You may find a motif is too small for your design or has too much background. After stabilizing it, choose a different piece of clothing to surround it to fit your needs. ------>

Or, if you have motifs too small for their own block, combine them with a T-shirt that needs a motif.

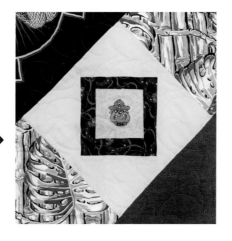

Motif Is Blending with the Background

If your motif blends into the background, surround it so that you have contrast. The white T-shirt was too close in color to the background fabric, so a pop of red did the trick.

Having Little and Big Motifs

Our *Friendship Star* quilt uses two block sizes, so you can take advantage of small and large motifs.

T-shirts will often have a small motif on the front and a larger motif on the back. The small motif from the front worked perfectly for the 9″ finished block.

The 13″ block uses a larger motif and was angled to fit within the parallelogram shape.

Using Clothing for Background Squares, Too

Our *Circle Gets the Square!* quilt uses motifs as well as clothing for the background squares, so you can make good use of all of your clothing. This is a good design to use if you have many different colors. The sashing helps to pull the design together. Find a neutral that will work.

Having Big Pieces

Joe's Quilt makes good use of larger pieces of clothing, such as men's shirts, ties, and large T-shirt motifs cut into half-square triangles. The half-square triangles in this quilt help to move the pattern and color around the quilt to create interest and flow.

Having No Motifs

Twinkle Star quilt uses clothing that doesn't necessarily have motifs. These are pajamas, little dresses, and onesie outfits.

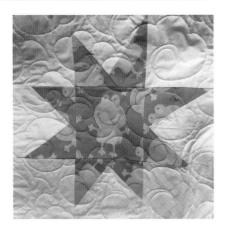

Motif Is Too Large

If the motif is too large and/or you want to be creative, cut the motif into triangles and distribute them throughout the quilt.

Or, if a motif is too large but you want to use an image of it in your quilt, consider taking a photo.

Adjust the size in a photo program and print it on fabric designed for home printers. Or use the services of Bags of Love (bagsoflove.com) or Spoonflower (spoonflower.com) to print the image. This is an appropriate solution if the T-shirt or clothing is just too precious to cut apart. You will have the image you need and can keep the clothing intact.

Having No Background on a Logo or Emblem

If you have an emblem from a sports team or club, you can stitch or fuse it to another fabric.

Using Clothes with Zippers

If the motif is on the front of a child's clothing with a zipper up the center, remove the zipper, sew the seam closed, and proceed.

Using Onesies

Even the smallest size of clothing can yield generous sections. This onesie is size 0–6 months. Removing the feet and sleeves (which can also be used) gives you about 15˝ × 18˝ of usable fabric.

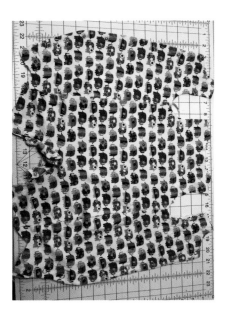

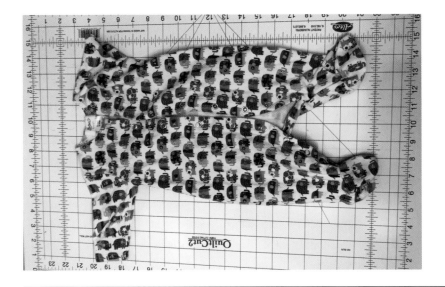

Having to Use Seams

If the pieces you want to cut would fit only if they overlap a seam, simply place the interfacing over the seam and press. The seam will be part of the block but will not be noticeable.

Having Digital Photos You Want to Use

Consider using photos of the person who will receive the quilt. A photo can be used as a motif in any of our designs.

Take a Look at All You Have

You likely will want to make some design decisions before you begin your quilt. Gather and analyze your T-shirts and clothing and choose a design that will make good use of them. Remember, you may need to supplement a design with other cotton fabrics.

T-Shirt Quilt Basics

Choosing a Stabilizer

T-shirt quilts would not be possible without the use of stabilizer. Applying interfacing or another stabilizer transforms otherwise unruly clothing into usable fabric. We have tried many different stabilizers and would like to share our favorites.

When T-shirt quilts became popular, the rule was to use a very stiff and heavy stabilizer on the shirts. However, this made for very stiff and heavy quilts. These days, there are many choices in stabilizers that keep the T-shirts pliable and soft.

Stabili-TEE Fusible Interfacing

Stabili-TEE (by C&T Publishing) is a lightweight fusible interfacing made specifically for stretchy, nonwoven T-shirt fabric as well as woven fabrics. It is 60″ wide and available in 2-yard packages or by the 10-yard bolt. It is easy to cut with a rotary cutter and ruler, a die-cutter, or scissors. The 60″ width is user-friendly for the piece sizes you'll need to make your T-shirt quilt. It stabilizes without too much thickness and stays flexible on the motif. It can be used on knits, silk ties, sweatshirts, and other stretchy fabrics.

931TD Fusible Midweight

This midweight interfacing by Pellon is made to be used on knits and wovens. It is 20″ wide and available by the yard. It is easy to cut with a rotary cutter and ruler, a die-cutter, or scissors. It stabilizes without too much thickness and stays flexible on the motif. It can be used on knits, silk ties, sweatshirts, and other stretchy fabrics.

Terial Magic

Terial Magic is a liquid fabric stabilizer in a spray bottle, intended to make fabric more paperlike and fray resistant. This amazing product temporarily stiffens fabric, making it easy to cut and sew. It can be left in or washed out. Terial Magic has a really nice, clean fragrance (sometimes helpful on used T-shirts). To use it, saturate the clothing pieces, hang to dry, and press with an iron. We suggest cutting the clothing pieces slightly larger than you need before applying Terial Magic. Follow the manufacturer's instructions and visit their website (terialmagic.com) for more information.

830 Easy Pattern

Easy Pattern (by Pellon) is a lightweight, nonfusible stabilizer that is 40″ wide and available by the yard. It is easy to cut with a rotary cutter and ruler, a die-cutter, or scissors. Sheer enough to trace through, Easy Pattern is intended for tracing clothing patterns. We used it for some of our templates and for foundation stitching. It can be left in your quilt—no removal necessary!

805 Wonder-Under or Steam-A-Seam 2

Wonder-Under (by Pellon) and Steam-A-Seam 2 (by the Warm Company) are fusible web products available by the yard. Wonder-Under is 20″ wide and Steam-a-Seam 2 comes in a variety of widths. Both products have release paper and include complete instructions. We used fusible web to create an appliqué from an emblem to be applied to the quilt with raw edges.

Applying Fusible Interfacing

1. Using a moderately hot iron and 2 pressing cloths (such as squares of muslin), take a few minutes to press the motif into shape. Place a pressing cloth down on the pressing board. Place the filleted motif right side down, taking care to smooth and straighten the motif. Often, T-shirts become misshapen; this is your chance to re-shape the motif a bit. Cover with another pressing cloth and press to flatten.

2. Center the fusible interfacing on the wrong side of the filleted motif. Place a damp pressing cloth on top or use the steam setting on your iron; press. Hold the iron down a few seconds and then lift and move to the next section of the motif. Check to make sure it is fused. If necessary, increase the temperature of the iron.

Remember, you don't need to worry about the grain of the fabric since you are stabilizing the T-shirt with fusible interfacing.

PRESSING TIPS

- Always start with a moderately hot iron. It is better to have to raise the temperature rather than over-heat the fusible.

- Do not press directly on the motifs or appliqués.

Scant ¼″ Seam Allowance

The seam allowance plays a major role in the accuracy of any quilting block. In most cases, an accurate ¼″ seam allowance works well. However, there are times when you need to consider sewing with a scant ¼″ seam allowance. Using clothing is one of those times because the thickness of the fabric and stabilizer may make your seams a bit thicker.

If your block has many pieces, it's understandable that each one of the seams will affect the finished size of the block. The thickness of your thread and the pressing of the seams to the side take up a slight bit of space, and by the time you have the block finished, you might be ⅛″–¼″ off. That may not sound like much, but over the entire quilt, it will add up. Using a scant ¼″ seam will help, as will pressing seams open.

What does a scant ¼″ seam allowance look like? It is a thread width smaller than a regular ¼″ seam allowance.

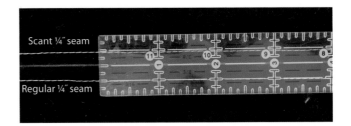

Pressing

It seems so simple … get your iron hot and go for it! However, think about the difference between pressing and ironing:

You *iron* your blouse with a back-and-forth movement of the iron to smooth wrinkles.

You *press* quilt seams. Place the iron down on the seam and press the heat into the fabric.

After you have pressed with an iron, it helps to follow up with a clapper (a tailoring tool) to further flatten the seams. While the seam is still warm, place the clapper on the seam and apply pressure for a few seconds. Repeat along the whole seam. The clapper flattens the seam for less bulk and helps to keep the block square and free from distortion.

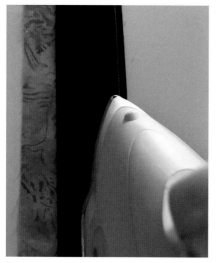
Press seam as sewn.

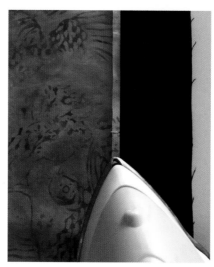
Open seam and press.

Flatten seam again by applying pressure with clapper while fabric is still warm.

Half-Square Triangles

Half-square triangles are square units made of 2 triangles. When using this technique to make half-square triangles, cut the squares 1″ larger than your finished square. This will slightly oversize the half-square triangle, giving you some leeway to trim the half-square triangle to the required size.

1. Layer 2 squares, right sides together. Draw a diagonal line from corner to corner on the lighter square. Pin together.

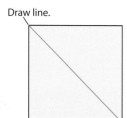
Draw line.

2. Sew a ¼″ seam on both sides of the drawn line.

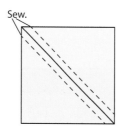
Sew.

3. Cut on the drawn line.

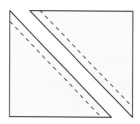

4. Press; then open and press the seam allowance toward the darker triangle. Trim each half-square triangle to the desired size.

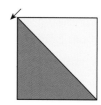

Borders

Many of our projects include optional borders. It is important to add borders correctly to keep your quilt squared and prepared for quilting and to eliminate bulk that often occurs when borders are added incorrectly. If the quilt is rectangular, add the long borders first.

Adding the Long Borders

1. To find the correct measurement of the long borders, find the center of each short side and measure from one side to the other. Measuring through the center will help to square your quilt if the 2 sides are different lengths. This measurement is the length of the left and right borders in our example.

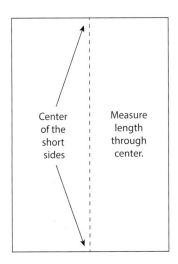

Center of the short sides / Measure length through center.

2. To construct borders longer than the width of the fabric, join the border strips together with a diagonal seam. Align 2 border strips perpendicular to one another, right sides together. With a ruler, draw a diagonal line for sewing and pin.

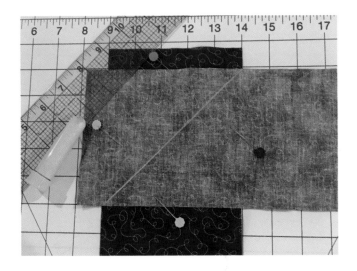

3. Sew along the diagonal line; then trim excess to ¼˝. Press the seams to one side.

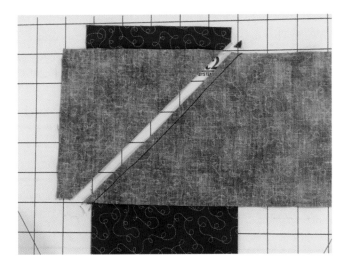

Cut the 2 borders to the measurement found in Step 1.

4. Determine the midpoints of both the border strips and the quilt top by folding them in half and placing a pin at the fold.

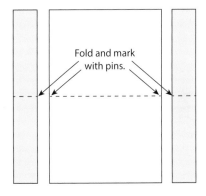

Fold and mark with pins.

> ### TIP
> On large quilts, it is helpful to find and pin two additional points on the quilt and border midway between the center and quilt edges for increased accuracy.

5. Lay the quilt on a flat surface. Right sides together, begin pinning the borders to the quilt top by lining up the center pins and the ends. Without stretching the border or the quilt, add pins to evenly align the border to the side of the quilt. If the border is longer than the side or vice versa, distribute the excess throughout the section.

6. Sew the borders to the quilt. Press the seams toward the border. *Always press from the right side of the quilt—never from the wrong side.* If you have a clapper, use it to flatten your seam.

Adding the Short Borders

1. To find the correct measurement of the short border, find the center of each long side and measure from side to side. This measurement is the length of the top and bottom borders in our example.

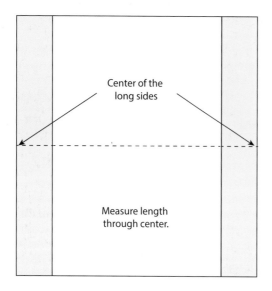

2. Using this measurement, construct and attach the short borders following Adding the Long Borders, Steps 2–6 (page 15).

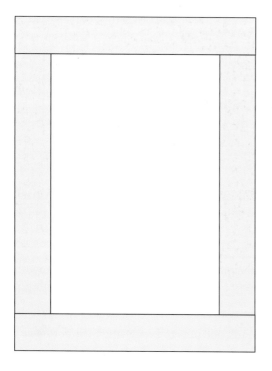

To add multiple borders, repeat the process for each round of borders.

Creating Labels

Labels are a great way to further personalize a quilt. Labels are a small detail that make a huge impact. They are the icing on the cake, adding that little something special.

Printed Labels

Labels can be printed on an inkjet printer. You can treat your fabric with Terial Magic (follow the instructions on the bottle) or purchase fabric that was pretreated for printing. Simply create the label on your computer and print.

Embroidered Labels

If you have access to an embroidery machine, consider using it to make your labels. Gary passed away last year, and his wife brought us his clothes to make a quilt. She also shared Gary's obituary with us, which began, "Gary, an extraordinary husband." We used the pocket of one of his shirts for the label.

Adding Tulle to Labels

When we received clothing from one of our customers, the bag included a tutu from a dance recital. Since tulle is not the heartiest fabric, we couldn't use it for a block. Instead, we framed the label with it and added a Red Sox logo from a tiny hat that didn't have a place on the quilt front.

Tie Labels

We also used the labels from a client's ties to create the label for the back of his tie quilt. They were too interesting not to include!

Labels don't need to be extravagant, but they are a nice way to take a T-shirt quilt to the next level.

TIPS FOR SUCCESS

- When pinning and sewing a background fabric to a T-shirt fabric, always have the T-shirt fabric on top. Different-weight fabrics need special care when sewing. With the T-shirt fabric on top, you can be sure the cut edges stay aligned while you sew.

- When you cut fusible interfacing, be sure that it is smaller than the size of the T-shirt or clothing. If it extends beyond, there's a chance it will be fused to your ironing surface.

- When applying fusible interfacing, don't be concerned about the grain of the fabric. Once the interfacing is fused to the fabric, the fabric will no longer stretch.

- If you encounter skipped stitches when sewing the T-shirt pieces, use a ballpoint needle.

- Take photos throughout the process. Sometimes a photo can tell you what needs to change or what is working. We take dozens of photos each time we design a new quilt.

- There are some limitations to the clothing you can use in a quilt. Knitted or crocheted items are a challenge to stabilize and would not be easy to use in a quilt.

- We have found that T-shirt quilts can be very heavy. Consider using wool or polyester batting, which does not add too much to the weight.

- Pockets can make great motifs! Consider sewing the pocket closed, though. On a wallhanging, it might be fun to be able to put items in the pockets. But on a bed quilt, the open pocket might catch on something and tear. Pockets also make great labels for your quilt.

- Do you have a great photo you want to include in a quilt? Use a printable fabric sheet, or consider Bags of Love (bagsoflove.com) or Spoonflower (spoonflower.com), great online resources that allow you to upload your photos to print on fabric. If you have something too precious to cut up for your quilt, take a photo and visit one of these sites. Your memento will remain intact.

Twinkle Star

Finished quilt: 61″ × 83″
Finished block: 5½″ × 5½″

Twinkle Star includes blocks that are less fussy than some of the other patterns in this book. We chose to use one piece of clothing to complete each star. If you prefer a scrappier look, however, mix the star centers with points from different clothing to create your own design. This design would work with T-shirts as well as clothing or a combination of both.

For those of you who like to jump ahead and follow your own directions (No judgment here—we do the same thing!), please notice that this quilt is constructed in rows, not star by star.

PLANNING THE STARS

To make your stars pop, use the same fabric for each star or partial star (see the quilt assembly diagram, page 22). You will need the following:

- 15 full stars with 8 points and 1 center

- 5 partial stars with 6 points and 1 center

- 1 corner star with 4 points and 1 center

- 5 star tips with 2 points and no center

You will be able to use smaller items of clothing for the partial stars.

Fabric and Stabilizer

Materials are based on 40″ usable width for purchased cotton fabric.

T-shirts or clothing: 21–25 items

Neutral solid or print: 4⅝ yards (This can be 1 fabric, scrappy, or an assortment of similar colors.)

Backing: 69″ × 91″

Binding: ⅝ yard

Stabilizer: 2⅜ yards of 60″-wide Stabili-TEE Fusible Interfacing (by C&T Publishing) or 6½ yards of 20″-wide light- to midweight fusible interfacing, *or* Terial Magic to treat your fabric

Batting: 69″ × 91″

Cutting

T-shirts or clothing: Prepare the clothing as explained in How to Fillet Clothing (page 7). See Construction (below) for further cutting details.

Neutral solid or print

Cut 11 strips 6″ × width of fabric.

- Subcut 62 squares 6″ × 6″ for the setting squares.

Cut 14 strips 6½″ × width of fabric.

- Subcut 82 squares 6½″ × 6½″ for the star points.

Binding: Cut 8 strips 2½″ × width of fabric.

Stabilizer: Cut 103 squares 6½″ × 6½″.

Construction

All seam allowances are a scant ¼″ unless noted otherwise. See Working with T-Shirts and Clothing (page 7) and T-Shirt Quilt Basics (page 12) for more information about the techniques used in this project.

Stabilizing and Cutting the Clothing

Note: For the full stars, you will need enough fabric from each T-shirt or article of clothing to cut 1 square 6″ × 6″ for the star center and 8 half-square triangles for the star points. The interfacing squares are oversize at 6½″ × 6½″ to allow for possible distortion. Depending on the size of the T-shirt or clothing pieces, you may be able to use 5 squares, 4 of which can then be cut diagonally for the star points. - - - - - - - - - - - ->

Or if the clothing is a smaller size, cut some of the interfacing squares in half diagonally and then creatively place the triangles where they fit on the clothing. ->

Square for star center

Square for star center

1. Arrange the interfacing squares or triangles, fusible side down, on the back of the T-shirt or other clothing fabric.

2. Fuse the interfacing to the clothing (refer to Applying Fusible Interfacing, page 13, or follow the manufacturer's instructions).

3. Use a rotary cutter and ruler to cut the following from the fused pieces:

• 1 square 6″ × 6″ for the star center

• 8 triangles for the star points. If you have not already cut the interfacing into triangles, trim the squares along the edge of the interfacing; then cut each in half diagonally (the triangles will be oversize).

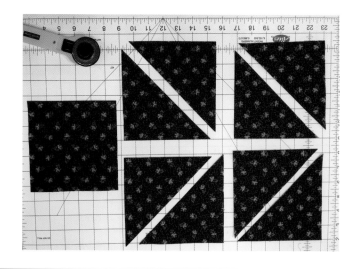

Assembling the Star Points

1. On adjacent sides of a background square 6½″ × 6½″, mark the centers with a crease. Pin a star triangle to the background square, right sides together, using the center mark for reference. You can place the triangle points just past the center or off-center to make the star points a little wonkier.

2. Make sure that the triangle extends beyond the center point of the background square. Fold the triangle back before sewing to confirm that the star point covers the entire background square.

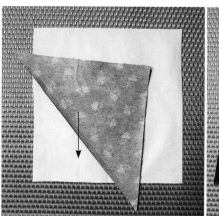

Correct placement

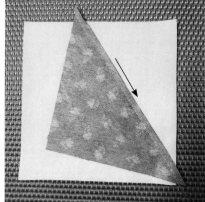

Incorrect placement. When flipped back, the point does not cover the background.

TIP

Changing the angle of the triangle will change the wonkiness of the point, making a more interesting star. As you can see, the star points can be large or small depending on the angle you choose for placing the triangle.

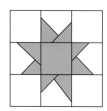

3. Using a ¼″ seam allowance, sew the triangle to the background fabric.

4. Trim the background even with the seam allowance and press toward the star point.

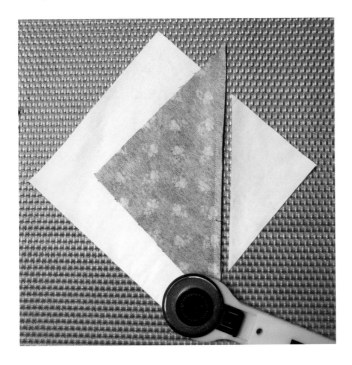

5. Trim the corner even with the background square.

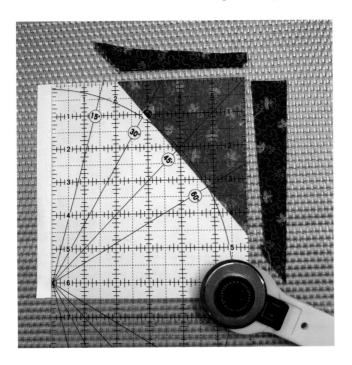

6. Place a second star point on the background, overlapping the existing star point at least ½″ from the edge. Pin.

7. Sew the triangle to the background fabric.

8. Trim the background fabric as in Step 4 and press to the star point.

9. Trim the block to 6″ × 6″ and set aside.

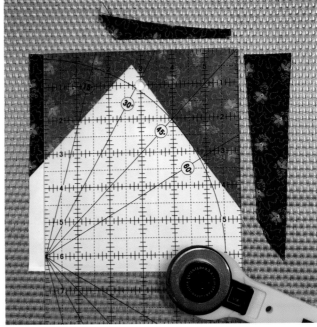

10. Repeat Steps 1–9 to make all the star points needed. Refer to Planning the Stars (page 19) for the number of points needed.

Quilt Assembly

Refer to the quilt assembly diagram (below).

1. We encourage you to lay out your quilt on a design wall, the floor, or even a bed to help to distribute the color throughout your quilt.

2. Sew the squares together in rows.

3. Press the seam allowances in the rows in alternate directions so that when the rows are sewn together, the seams will nest.

4. Sew the rows together.

5. Layer, baste, quilt, bind, and enjoy!

TIPS

• Since this quilt is assembled row by row, your star points and centers will be in separate pieces as you plan the layout. It may be helpful to pin each star together in order to more easily rearrange as you design. Once the design has been finalized, remove the pins.

• Distribute your colors thoughtfully! Most of our clothing was bright and colorful, so we balanced the brights with more muted colors.

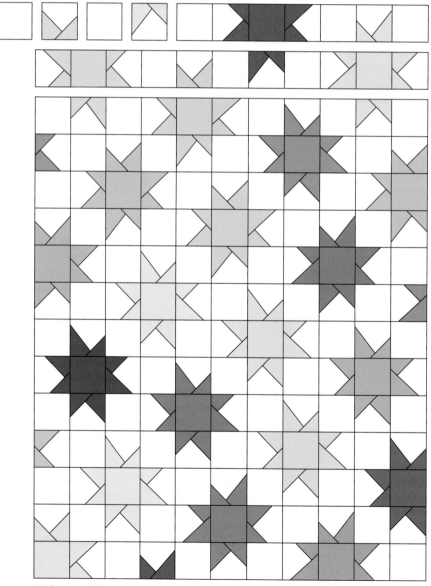

Quilt assembly

Hog Heaven

Finished quilt: 96½˝ × 96½˝
Finished block: 32˝ × 32˝

Hog Heaven was made for Linda, a fun-loving Harley-Davidson–riding friend of our family. Linda travels all over the country to attend Harley-Davidson events and has collected T-shirts along the way. She wasn't interested in wearing the shirts, so a T-shirt quilt was a great way to display her memorabilia.

Harley-Davidson T-shirt motifs are generally very large, so our design needed to include large squares to accommodate their size. We found two colorful coordinating fabrics to complement the T-shirts and give the quilt some pizazz, and chose a black background to set our design.

Fabric and Stabilizer

Materials are based on 40″ usable width for purchased cotton fabric.

T-shirts: 9 with large motifs

Black: 5½ yards for background and binding (Choose a color that blends with your motif fabrics.)

Multicolor print: 1⅞ yards for star points

Orange print: 1⅜ yards for star points

Backing: 105″ × 105″

Stabilizer: 1¾ yards of 60″-wide Stabili-TEE Fusible Interfacing (by C&T Publishing) or 4¾ yards of 20″-wide light- to midweight fusible interfacing, *or* Terial Magic to treat your T-shirts

Batting: 105″ × 105″

> ### NOTE
> It will be easier to center the motifs if you have a 16½″ × 16½″ square acrylic ruler, but it is not necessary. If you don't have this size of ruler, consider cutting a 16½″ × 16½″ square from nonfusible stabilizer, such as Pellon's 830 Easy Pattern (page 13), to help center your motifs when trimming them to size.

Cutting

T-shirts: Prepare the T-shirts as explained in How to Fillet Clothing (page 7). See Construction (below) for cutting instructions.

Black

Cut 10 strips 9½″ × width of fabric.

- Subcut 40 squares 9½″ × 9½″ for the star-point backgrounds.

Cut 7 strips 8½″ × width of fabric.

- Subcut 28 squares 8½″ × 8½″ for the setting squares.

Cut 11 strips 2½″ × width of fabric for the binding.

Multicolor print

Cut 6 strips 9½″ × width of fabric.

- Subcut 24 squares 9½″ × 9½″.

Orange print

Cut 4 strips 9½″ × width of fabric.

- Subcut 16 squares 9½″ × 9½″.

Stabilizer: Cut 9 squares 18″ × 18″.

Construction

All seam allowances are a scant ¼″ unless noted otherwise. See Working with T-Shirts and Clothing (page 7) and T-Shirt Quilt Basics (page 12) for more information about the techniques used in this project.

Stabilizing and Cutting the Clothing

1. Fuse an interfacing square 18″ × 18″ to the back of each T-shirt motif.

2. From the right side of the T-shirt, center a 16½″ × 16½″ ruler or nonfusible stabilizer square 16½″ × 16½″ on the motif. Cut the square from the stabilized T-shirts.

Star Point Assembly

1. Make 48 half-square triangles using 24 black squares 9½″ × 9½″ and 24 multicolor print squares 9½″ × 9½″. Trim to 8½″ × 8½″ square. Refer to Half-Square Triangles (page 14).

2. Using the remaining 16 black squares 9½″ × 9½″ and 16 orange print squares 9½″ × 9½″ to make 32 half-square triangles. Trim to 8½″ × 8½″ square.

> ### NOTE
> If your star-point colors are striped fabrics and you would like to control the direction of the stripes, refer to *Friendship Star*, Star Corners (page 54) for creating directional half-square triangles.

Determine a Layout

Before you begin assembling your blocks, decide on a layout (refer to the quilt assembly diagram, page 26). It is important to balance the position of the T-shirts' colors and motifs for an appealing design. The layout will determine how each block is assembled. Label each motif with its block number: From left to right, 1–3 on the top row, 4–6 on the second row, and 7–9 on the bottom row.

Block Assembly

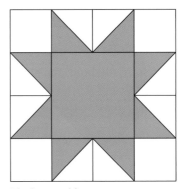

Block assembly

Blocks 1, 3, 5, 7, and 9

1. For each block, gather the center motif square, 4 black squares 8½″ × 8½″, and 8 multicolor half-square triangles.

2. Referring to the block assembly diagram, stitch the blocks together in rows; then sew the rows together.

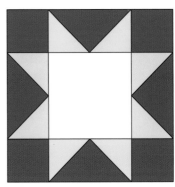

Blocks 1, 3, 5, 7, and 9

Blocks 2, 4, 6, and 8

1. For each block, gather the center motif square, 2 black squares 8½″ × 8½″, 8 orange half-square triangles, and 2 multicolor half-square triangles.

2. Referring to the block assembly diagram for each block, stitch the blocks together in rows; then sew the rows together.

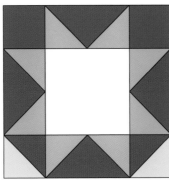

Block 2

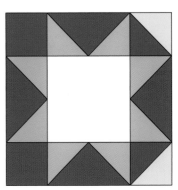

Block 4

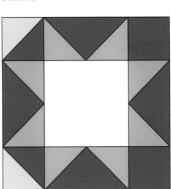

Block 6

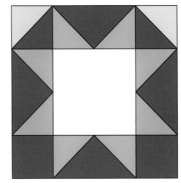

Block 8

Quilt Assembly

1. Referring to the quilt assembly diagram (below), sew the blocks together in rows.

2. Sew the rows together.

3. Layer, baste, quilt, bind, and enjoy!

Quilt assembly

Joe's Quilt

Finished quilt: 58½″ × 58½″
Finished block: 13″ × 13″

The blocks in *Joe's Quilt* are very simple to make. The Square-in-a-Square (in-a-Square!) is a very forgiving block. The squares float and the points remain intact, even if you are a beginner. When the blocks are sewn together, they become an eye-catching quilt.

Follow these instructions to create individual blocks. Our quilt has sixteen blocks, but you decide how many will work for your quilt.

Fabric and Stabilizer

Materials are based on 40˝ usable width for purchased cotton fabric.

You can use T-shirts or clothing for any or all of the fabrics in this quilt. If you are using knits, stabilize the fabric before cutting. If you are using cotton fabrics or other fabrics that do not stretch, stabilizer is not necessary. Refer to Choosing a Stabilizer (page 12) for more information. The yardage for the teal print and dark teal fabrics is enough to make 16 blocks without using clothing for Round 2.

T-shirts or clothing with motifs that will fit into a 4½˝ finished square: 1 motif for each block center (We used 16 motifs.)

Assorted prints: 1 fat eighth or ¼ yard for each block, for first round of triangles around center square (We used 16 prints.)

Teal print: 1¼ yards

Dark teal: 1¼ yards

Border and binding: 1¼ yards

Backing: 67˝ × 67˝

Stabilizer: ½ yard of 60˝-wide Stabili-TEE Fusible Interfacing (by C&T Publishing) or 1¼ yards of 20˝-wide light- to midweight fusible interfacing, *or* Terial Magic to treat your T-shirts for the center motifs only

Optional: If you use T-shirts or other knit fabric for the centers and Round 2, you will need 2 yards of Stabili-TEE *or* 5¼ yards of 20˝-wide interfacing.

Batting: 67˝ × 67˝

Cutting

T-shirts or clothing with motifs: Prepare the clothing as explained in How to Fillet Clothing (page 7). Add stabilizer to the knit fabrics before cutting.

• Cut 1 square 5˝ × 5˝, with the motif centered, for each block.

Assorted prints

From each fat eighth:

Cut 2 squares 6˝ × 6˝ for each block; subcut each in half diagonally to yield 4 triangles.

Optional: If you are using knit clothing, wait until you add the stabilizer (see Stabilizer, below).

Teal print and dark teal: Cut 1 square 8½˝ × 8½˝ from each fabric for Round 2 of each block; subcut each in half diagonally to yield 4 triangles. (If you use 1 fabric, cut 2 squares for each block.)

Border and binding

See Borders (page 15) and wait until you have pieced and measured your quilt top before you cut the borders. The following sizes match the project quilt.

Cut 6 strips 3½˝ × width of fabric for the border.

Cut 7 strips 2½˝ × width of fabric for the binding.

Stabilizer

Cut only the number of pieces needed for T-shirts or knit fabric.

Cut 1 square 5˝ × 5˝ for the block center.

Cut 2 squares 6˝ × 6˝ for Round 1 (for the square around the motif).

Cut 2 squares 8½˝ × 8½˝ for Round 2.

Construction

All seam allowances are a scant ¼˝ unless noted otherwise. See Working with T-Shirts and Clothing (page 7) and T-Shirt Quilt Basics (page 12) for more information about the techniques used in this project.

Plan Your Quilt

To begin, you will need to make some design decisions.

• Determine the number of blocks based on the number of motifs you have.

• There are 3 squares in each block—a center (the motif), a middle square, and an outer square. Pair each motif with a complementary or contrasting fabric for the middle square, which is Round 1.

The decision on the outer square, Round 2, can be made later, but start thinking about fabrics you might use. In our quilt, we chose 2 fabrics for each block, but we used the same fabrics throughout to unify the design.

Block Assembly, Round 1

1. Choose 1 center square 5″ × 5″ and 4 matching triangles (cut from a pair of 6″ × 6″ squares) for Round 1.

2. Find the center of one side of the square and the long side of a triangle. Mark with a pin or crease.

3. Pin right sides together, lining up the centers.

4. Sew using a ¼″ seam allowance. Press toward the center square.

5. Repeat Steps 2–4 on the opposite side of the center square.

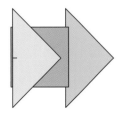

6. Press the seams toward the square. Trim off the ears even with the square.

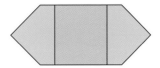

7. To complete the square-within-a-square block, repeat Steps 2–6 to sew the remaining triangles to the other sides of the center square. Press these seams away from the center square.

8. Trim the block to 8½″ × 8½″ square, centering the motif square.

9. Repeat Steps 1–8 to make 16 blocks.

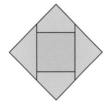

> **NOTE**
> Remember, this block is very forgiving and can be trimmed larger or smaller, if necessary, for uniformly sized blocks.

Block Assembly, Round 2

1. Repeat Block Assembly, Round 1, Steps 1–7 (at left and above) with the Round 1 block as the center and 4 matching triangles (cut from a pair of 8½″ × 8½″ squares).

2. Trim the block to 13½″ × 13½″, making sure the motif is centered.

3. Repeat Steps 1 and 2 to make 16 blocks.

Quilt Assembly

You may have a different number of blocks, so adjust the layout accordingly.

1. The quilt is assembled in rows. Sew 4 blocks together in a row; press the seams in opposite directions for each row.

2. Sew the rows together.

3. See Borders (page 15) to check your quilt measurements and adjust your border lengths as needed.

4. Sew the border strips together diagonally to make 2 side borders 3½″ × 52½″ and 2 top and bottom borders 3½″ × 58½″.

5. Sew the side borders to the quilt first and then the top and bottom borders. Press the seams toward the borders.

6. Layer, baste, quilt, bind, and enjoy!

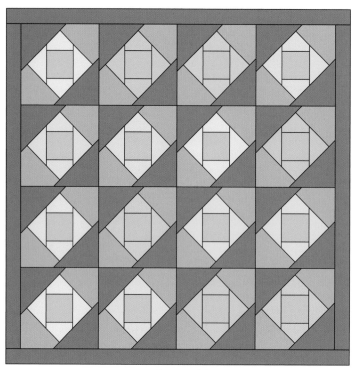

Quilt assembly

DESIGN TIPS

• If your logos are too small to fit the 5″ squares, follow our example and add a border to the logo. Two of the logos were small and needed a border. It was a good opportunity to use a few ties.

• Consider using some of the clothing more than once. Repeating some fabrics helps move your eye around the quilt.

• Consider cutting a motif diagonally; then use the partial motif around the center square in Round 2. This gives some texture to the block and makes you look twice.

Most of our choices for Round 2 were plain, solid shirts, with the exception of a few very large logos that would otherwise not fit in the quilt. The partial motifs were distributed around the quilt for interest.

Circle Gets the Square!

Circle Gets the Square! features motifs from 30 different clothing items. The background squares behind each circle also were cut from clothing. This pattern can be altered to accommodate the number of motifs you have and the circle size you use. You also may choose to use cotton fabrics as backgrounds instead of clothing.

We originally struggled with the clothing we had to make this quilt because there was such a variety of color and pattern. We decided to pair our motifs with our backgrounds before we took scissors to any of the clothing. We realized there was some clothing with distinctive patterns that should repeat twice or three times throughout the quilt. Don't be discouraged if the clothing doesn't look cohesive at this point. You can choose a sashing to bring it all together once you've created your blocks.

Fabric and Stabilizer

Materials are based on 40″ usable width for purchased cotton fabric.

T-shirts and clothing:

30 motifs that will fit within a 7″ circle

30 background squares 10″ × 10″ (These can be from T-shirts, clothing, fabric, or a combination.)

> ### TIP
>
> If the T-shirt or clothing piece is too small for a 7″ circle, consider piecing another section from the clothing to make it larger—it will not be noticeable. This process is explained in How to Fillet Clothing (page 7).

Outer border and sashing: 2⅝ yards

Cornerstones, inner border, and binding: 1⅛ yards

Backing: 78″ × 90″

Stabilizers: Our quilt is a combination of a few cotton dresses used as background squares that did not require stabilizer, and many stretchy onesies, pajamas, and T-shirts that did require stabilizer.

In the background, you will need stabilizers only if you are using T-shirts, knit, or other stretchy clothing. We used 3 stabilizers:

• Terial Magic for all motifs (You can substitute 1⅓ yards of Stabili-TEE Fusible Interfacing [by C&T Publishing] *or* 3⅝ yards of 20″-wide light- to midweight fusible interfacing.)

• 1⅝ yards of 45″-wide nonfusible stabilizer, such as Pellon's 830 Easy Pattern (page 13), for circles

• 1¾ yards of 60″-wide Stabili-TEE Fusible Interfacing or 4½ yards of 20″-wide light- to midweight fusible interfacing for background squares

Batting: 78″ × 90″

Template plastic: 1 sheet 8½″ × 11″

Cutting

Make a template for the 7″ circle (page 36) by tracing it onto template plastic, including the 1″ center circle. Cut along the outer traced line.

Outer border and sashing

Cut 18 strips 2½″ × width of fabric; subcut 71 rectangles 2½″ × 10″ for the sashing.

Cut 8 strips 5″ × width of fabric for the outer border.

Cornerstones, inner border, and binding

Cut 12 strips 2½″ × width of fabric; set aside 9 strips for the binding. From the remaining 3 strips, subcut 42 squares 2½″ × 2½″ for the cornerstones.

Cut 7 strips 1″ × width of fabric for the inner border.

Stabilizers

Cut only the number of pieces needed for T-shirts or stretchy fabric.

Stabili-TEE Fusible Interfacing or other light- to midweight fusible interfacing (if not using Terial Magic)

Cut 30 squares 10″ × 10″ for the background squares.

Cut 30 squares 8″ × 8″ for the motifs.

Nonfusible stabilizer

Cut 30 squares 8″ × 8″ for the circle templates.

Construction

All seam allowances are a scant ¼˝ unless noted otherwise. See Working with T-Shirts and Clothing (page 7) and T-Shirt Quilt Basics (page 12) for more information about the techniques used in this project.

Plan the Quilt Layout

It may seem premature to decide on a layout before you have constructed the blocks, but taking this step will allow for changes to better your design. Deciding on a layout can be the most fun or most frustrating part of the quilt! We had such a variety of patterns and colors within our clothing. We determined that as long as each block looked pleasing, the blocks could be brought together by the sashing.

1. Pair each circle fabric with a background fabric.

2. Arrange the pairs. Don't be afraid to swap them around until you have a layout that is pleasing to your eye. Balance similar colors and patterns throughout the quilt.

3. Once you have determined a layout, pin each pair together to keep track of which circle goes with which background square.

4. Take pictures! That way you can take the pairs apart to stabilize.

Prepare the Background Squares

If you are using yardage for your background squares, or if your clothing is not a stretchy fabric like a T-shirt, stabilizer is not needed.

1. For background squares that do not need stabilizer, cut 10˝ × 10˝ squares.

2. For background squares that need stabilizer, fuse the interfacing square 10˝ × 10˝ to the back of the clothing. Trim to 10˝ × 10˝ square.

Construct the Circles

1. Prepare each motif with Terial Magic or apply the fusible interfacing as explained in Choosing a Stabilizer (page 12). At this point, do not fussy cut the motif circle.

2. Using a template made from the 7˝ circle pattern (page 36), trace the circle on each 8˝ square of nonfusible stabilizer. Include the 1˝ circle in the center.

TIP

If your motifs are larger or smaller than a 7˝ circle allows, adjust the size by tracing any circle you have on hand (a plate, a bowl). There are no hard-and-fast rules for the size of the circle in this design, as long as it is pleasing to your eye. Did you see the dog block in the bottom right corner of our quilt? He didn't fit in a 7˝ circle, so we made it slightly bigger to accommodate the entire motif. You didn't even notice, did you?

3. Place the motif fabric faceup and center the nonfusible stabilizer square 8″ × 8″ on top, centering the motif within the drawn circle. Use the open circle in the center of the drawn circle to help you line up the center of the circle with the center of the motif. (This is a tip we figured out after we made this first quilt, so there's no center circle in these photos.) Pin generously.

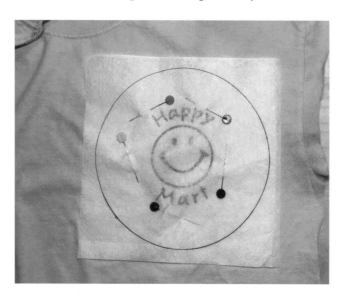

4. Stitch directly on the line around the entire circle. Begin and end with a backstitch.

5. Cut out the circle ¼″ outside the sewing line.

6. Cut 4 slits in the stabilizer, north/south and east/west, taking care not to cut through the motif.

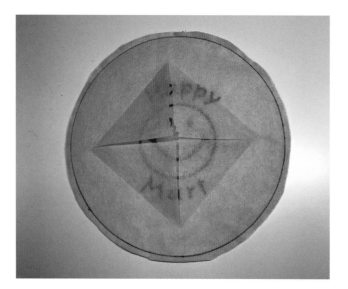

7. Turn the circle right side out. Using a pressing sheet, press from the stabilizer side; then flip and press from the front.

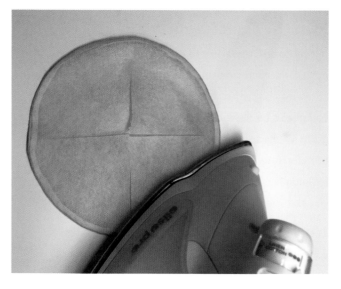

8. Repeat Steps 1–7 for each circle.

Block Assembly

1. Center the circle on the background square. Generously pin the circle to the background square.

2. Stitch around the edge of the circle using a decorative stitch on your sewing machine. We used the buttonhole stitch.

3. Repeat Steps 1 and 2 for each block.

Quilt Assembly

1. Referring to the quilt assembly diagram (at right), arrange your quilt with sashing and cornerstones.

2. Sew the vertical sashing between the blocks and to the right and left end of each row. Press the seams in each row in one direction.

3. Join the cornerstones and horizontal sashing in each row. Press the seams in the opposite direction to the Step 2 rows.

4. Sew the rows together. Press the seams in one direction.

5. See Borders (page 15) to check your quilt measurements and adjust your border lengths as needed.

6. Sew the 1″ inner border strips together diagonally to make 2 side borders 1″ × 71½″ and 2 top and bottom borders 1″ × 62″, or use your measurements.

7. Sew the side borders to the quilt first and then the top and bottom inner borders. Press the seams toward the borders.

8. Sew the 5″ outer border strips together diagonally to make 2 side borders 5″ × 72½″ and 2 top and bottom borders 5″ × 70″, or use your measurements.

9. Repeat Step 7 to add the outer borders.

10. Layer, baste, quilt, bind, and enjoy!

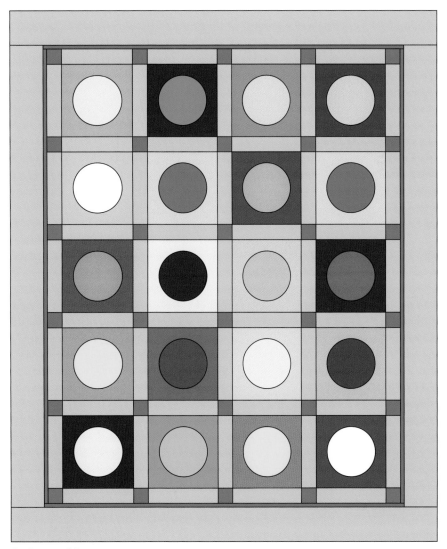

Quilt assembly

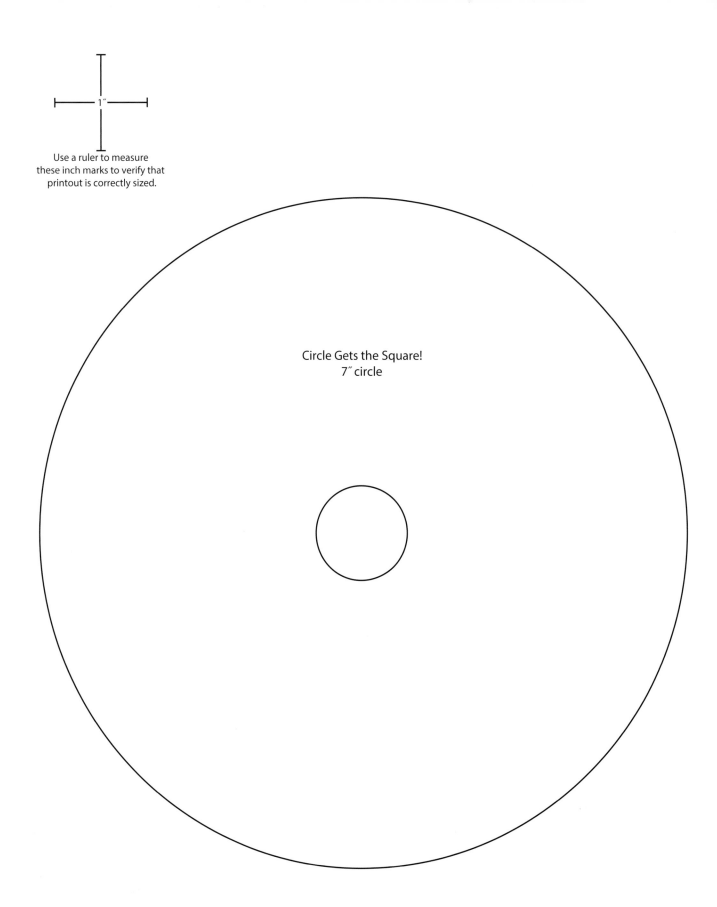

Use a ruler to measure these inch marks to verify that printout is correctly sized.

Circle Gets the Square!
7″ circle

Pile of Hexies

Finished quilt: 56½″ × 58½″
Finished block: 10″ × 6½

Our *Pile of Hexies* is a simple pattern with an eye-catching layout. We have found that many large motifs fit nicely in the hexagon shape. We've included a 6½″ finished-size hexagon pattern. Any size hexagon can be used, depending on the size of the motifs on your clothing.

Fabric and Stabilizer

Materials are based on 40˝ usable width for purchased cotton fabric.

T-shirts or clothing: 38 hexagons and 4 half-hexagons (Of course, you can change the size of your quilt to use however many hexies you wish.)

> **TIP**
>
> If you do not have clothing with motifs that fit in the half hexagons, consider floating that row by using a rectangle of background fabric in place of the half hexagon.

Green print: 4 yards for the background, border, and binding (This is a generous measurement, allowing for extra fillers if you decide to substitute the background instead of the half-hexagons.)

Backing: 65˝ × 67˝

Stabilizer: 1¼ yards of 60˝-wide Stabili-TEE Fusible Interfacing (by C&T Publishing) or 4 yards of 20˝-wide fusible interfacing, *or* Terial Magic to treat your T-shirts

Batting: 65˝ × 67˝

Template plastic: 1 sheet 12˝ × 18˝

> **TIP**
>
> If the size of our hexagon does not work for your motifs, enlarge or reduce it using a photocopier or scanner. Adjust the size of the rectangles accordingly. You can cut a hexagon template up to 12˝ tall from a 12˝ × 18˝ sheet of template plastic.

Cutting

Make templates for the hexagon and half-hexagon (page 41) by tracing them onto template plastic. Trace the bold line and seam allowance.

T-shirts or clothing: Prepare the clothing as explained in How to Fillet Clothing (page 7).

Green print

These half-rectangles will be added to the 4 corners of each hexagon to form a large rectangle. The hexagon floats within the rectangle, so the corners are oversized.

Cut 9 strips 7½˝ × width of fabric; subcut 80 rectangles 7½˝ × 4¼˝.

Cut 8 strips 3½˝ × width of fabric for the border.

Cut 7 strips 2½˝ × width of fabric for the binding.

Stabilizer: Trace the hexagon template onto the fusible interfacing, leaving about ½˝ between hexagons. Cut apart about ¼˝ outside the hexagon lines.

Construction

All seam allowances are a scant ¼˝ unless noted otherwise. See Working with T-Shirts and Clothing (page 7) and T-Shirt Quilt Basics (page 12) for more information about the techniques used in this project.

Stabilizing and Cutting the Clothing

1. Fuse the interfacing with the drawn hexagon to the wrong side of each motif, centering the motif inside the hexagon.

2. Recheck the hexagon by placing the template on the fusible interfacing to make sure the pressing has not distorted the hexagon. If it did, redraw the lines.

3. Use a rotary cutter and ruler to cut out the stabilized hexagon on the drawn lines.

> **TIP**
>
> If you cannot see the motif from the wrong side, turn the motif right side up and use the hexagon template or the interfacing hexagon to mark the edges of the motif with pins. Turn the motif to the wrong side and position the interfacing with the drawn hexagon covering the pinned area. Carefully remove the pins from the right side and fuse the interfacing in place.

Block Assembly

1. Divide the rectangles 7½″ × 4¼″ into 2 equal piles, all right side up. Subcut one pile in half diagonally as shown in the right triangle diagram below and the remaining pile in half diagonally as shown in the left triangle diagram. You will need 2 right triangles and 2 left triangles for each block.

Right triangle   Left triangle

2. Make a mark or place a pin on the wrong side of 2 right triangles and 2 left triangles, ½″ from the corner along the angled side.

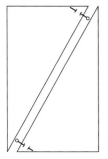

3. Right sides together, pair a right triangle and the top right side of the hexagon. Align the ½″ mark with the top right corner of the hexagon. Pin and stitch the triangle to the hexagon.

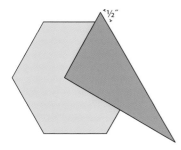

4. Press the seam to the triangle.

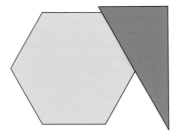

5. Repeat Steps 3 and 4 with the other right triangle on the lower left corner of the hexagon.

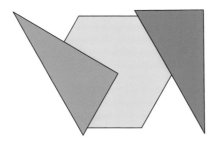

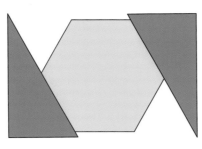

6. Trim the triangles even with the next edges of the hexagon.

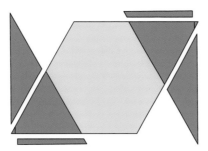

7. Repeat Steps 3–6 to join a left triangle to the top left and lower right corners of the hexagon.

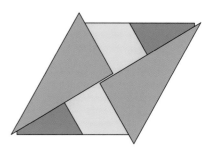

8. The rectangles will be oversize. You may want to complete all of the blocks and check for a common size before you trim them to a rectangle. Our rectangles were trimmed to 10½″ × 7″.

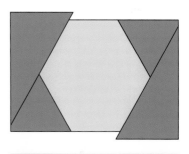

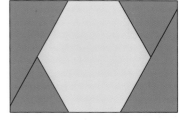

9. Before you make the half-hexagons into rectangles, you may want to wait until you have done the first step of Quilt Assembly (page 40) to see where you want to place your half-hexagon motifs. Use the same process as in Block Assembly to add triangles to the top corners or the bottom corners of the half-hexagon motif.

Quilt Assembly

1. Referring to the quilt assembly diagram (below), arrange the blocks in a pleasing design, distributing the colors to balance the quilt.

2. Sew the first column of rectangles together. Press the seam allowances down.

3. Sew the second column of rectangles together, beginning and ending with a half-hexagon. Press the seam allowances up.

4. Repeat Steps 2 and 3 until all columns are sewn together.

5. Sew the columns together and press the seam allowances to one side.

6. See Borders (page 15) to check your quilt measurements and adjust your border lengths.

7. Sew the border strips together diagonally end to end to make 2 side borders 3½″ × 52½″ and 2 top and bottom borders 3½″ × 56½″, or use your measurements.

8. Sew the side borders to the quilt first and then the top and bottom borders. Press the seams toward the borders.

9. Layer, baste, quilt, bind, and enjoy!

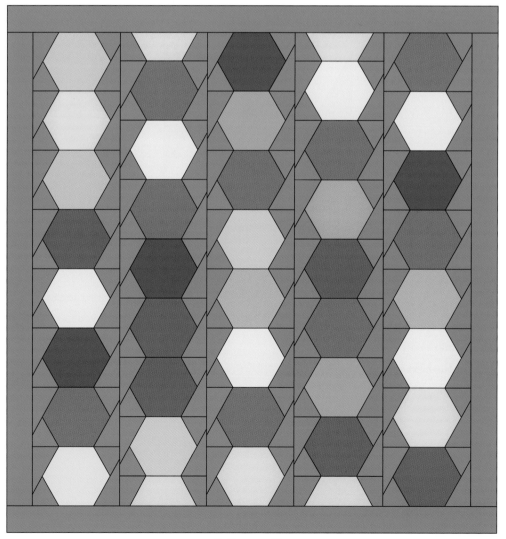

Quilt assembly

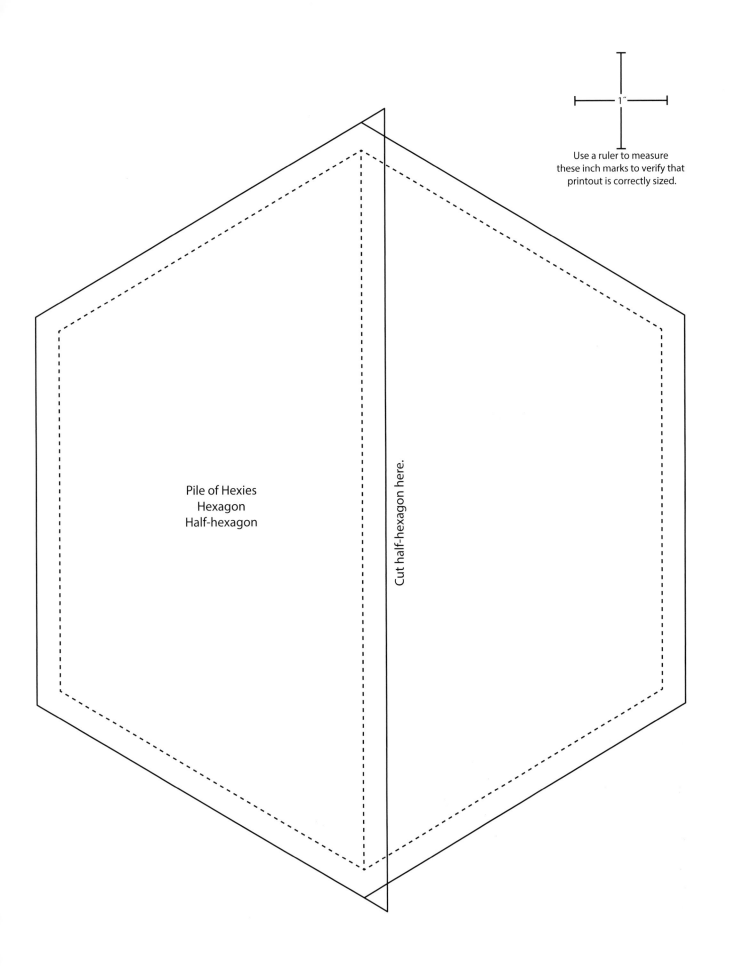

Use a ruler to measure these inch marks to verify that printout is correctly sized.

1"

Pile of Hexies
Hexagon
Half-hexagon

Cut half-hexagon here.

That's My Life!

Finished quilt: 71″ × 90½″
Finished block: 13″ × 22½″

That's My Life! is a T-shirt quilt made for a family friend, Caroline, for her graduation from high school. It documents her middle and high school years, including shirts from field hockey (varsity captain!), swimming, basketball, softball, class plays, and other great memories. When Caroline saw the quilt for the first time, she exclaimed, "That's my life!" An enthusiastic reaction does wonders for the quiltmakers, and we were thrilled that she loved it. This is the perfect design for those T-shirts with larger motifs. We made the quilt with eight vertical motifs and six horizontal motifs. You may need to vary the size and layout based on the number of shirts and the orientation of the motifs. There are many options using the diamond shape, since each diamond is made into a rectangular block. The blocks can be sewn together using any layout pleasing to you.

Fabric and Stabilizer

Materials are based on 40″ usable width for purchased cotton fabric.

T-shirts: Our quilt used 14 T-shirts with motifs that fit in a 13″ × 22½″ diamond, either horizontally or vertically. If your motifs are smaller, see the cutting instructions for how to create a smaller diamond template.

Green print: 7 yards for background, border, and binding (This is a generous measurement, allowing for sashing and fillers if necessary.)

Backing: 79″ × 99″

Stabilizer:

3⅓ yards of 60″-wide Stabili-TEE Fusible Interfacing (by C&T Publishing) or 10 yards of 20″-wide light- to midweight fusible interfacing, *or* Terial Magic to treat your T-shirts

15″ × 26″ rectangle of lightweight nonwoven, nonfusible stabilizer for template

Batting: 79″ × 99″

60° triangle ruler: At least 12″ or larger, *or* make a template from the half-triangle pattern (page 50).

CREATING A 60° DIAMOND TEMPLATE

To create our template, we used the 12″ Clearview Triangle 60° Acrylic Ruler (by C&T Publishing). You can use any similar 60° triangle ruler or the half-triangle pattern (page 50). Note: *This template will be used for placement only. You will use the 60° ruler for cutting.*

1. Fold the rectangle of lightweight nonwoven, nonfusible stabilizer in half so it measures approximately 15″ × 13″. Place the triangle ruler on the stabilizer, lining up the 11¾″ line with the fold.

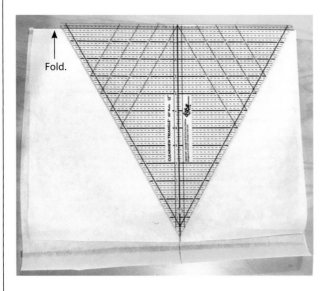
Fold.

2. Using a rotary cutter, trim around 2 angled sides of the triangle's outer edge (do not cut your template in half!). Remove the ruler and unfold for a diamond-shaped template.

NOTE

For a smaller diamond, determine the dimensions needed for the motifs. Line up the fold with a smaller measurement on the ruler, which will create a smaller diamond.

3. Using a permanent marker and a ruler, draw perpendicular lines on the template from tip to tip. The intersection of these lines will help you determine the center of the motifs.

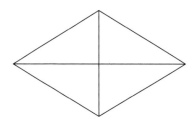

NOTE

To use the half-triangle pattern (page 50), join the pieces to make the half-triangle. Fold the rectangle of stabilizer in half twice so it measures approximately 15″ × 6½″. Align the corner of the pattern to the folded corner and trace the angled edge to make the diamond template.

TIP

If your only 60° ruler has a blunt tip instead of a pointed tip, you can use it to cut the diamond but will need to adjust the cutting line. To compensate for the loss of the ¼″ tip at the top of the ruler, line up the 11½″ line with the fold and extend the angled lines to create a point at the top.

Cutting

T-shirts: Prepare the clothing as explained in How to Fillet Clothing (page 7). Don't forget—if the template is larger than your T-shirt, you can add a portion from another section of the T-shirt to make it large enough for the diamond. See Construction (below) for further cutting details.

Green print

Cut 14 strips 9″ × width of fabric; subcut 28 rectangles 9″ × 15⅜″.

Cut 8 strips 6½″ × width of fabric for the outside horizontal sashing and borders.

Cut 6 strips 5½″ × width of fabric for the vertical sashing.

Cut 9 strips 2½″ × width of fabric for the binding.

Stabilizer: Cut 14 rectangles 15″ × 24″.

Construction

All seam allowances are a scant ¼″ unless noted otherwise. See Working with T-Shirts and Clothing (page 7) and T-Shirt Quilt Basics (page 12) for more information about the techniques used in this project.

Stabilizing and Cutting the Clothing

1. Before you add the interfacing, place the template on the right side of the T-shirt or other clothing to evaluate the placement of the motifs within the diamond. Use the perpendicular lines to pinpoint the center. Use pins to mark the points of the template on the motif fabric.

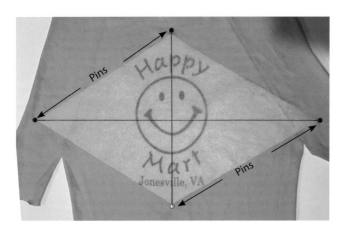

2. Turn the T-shirt over to the wrong side. Using a permanent marker, draw a dot where you see each pin. Remove the pins.

3. Press a fusible interfacing rectangle to the wrong side of the T-shirt, making sure you have covered the dots that indicate the outside edges of your template.

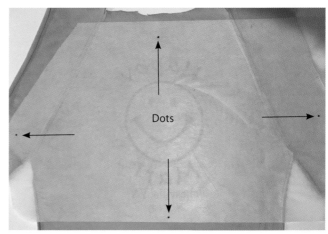

4. Once fused, replace the pins at the dots.

5. Turn the motif faceup and center the template where the pins indicate the corners of the diamond. Pin the template to the motif using flower-head pins so that you can align a ruler on top of the pins in the next step. Remove the pins from the wrong side.

6. Align the triangle ruler with one-half of the diamond. Using a rotary cutter, trim around 2 sides of the diamond's outer edge (do not cut your motif in half!). Rotate the ruler to trim the other 2 sides of the diamond.

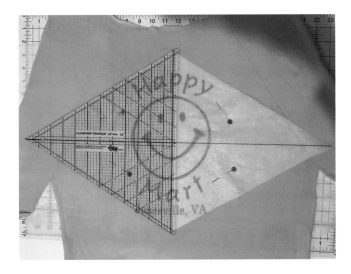
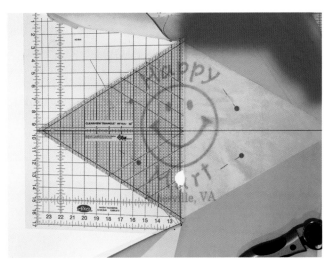
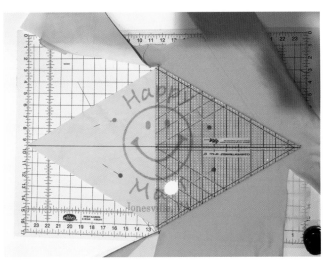
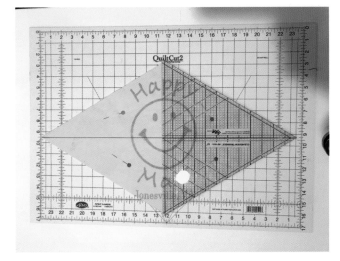
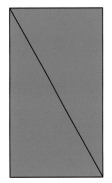

Block Assembly

All seams are ¼˝ unless noted otherwise.

1. Divide the rectangles 9˝ × 15⅜˝ in 2 equal piles, *all right side up.* Subcut one pile in half diagonally as shown in the right triangle diagram (at right) and the remaining pile in half diagonally as shown in the left triangle diagram. You will need 2 right triangles and 2 left triangles for each block.

Right triangle   Left triangle

These half-rectangles will be added to the 4 corners of each diamond to form a large rectangle. The diamond is floating within the rectangle, so the corners are oversized. *Note:* If your diamonds are a different size from the pattern, you will need to adjust the triangle size as well.

2. Gather 1 diamond, 2 right triangles, and 2 left triangles. The right triangles will be sewn to the top right and lower left corners of the diamond; the left triangles will be sewn to the top left and lower right corners.

3. Fold each side of the diamond in half and place a pin to mark the center. Fold the long side of each triangle in half, again marking the center with a pin.

4. Pair a triangle with a side of the diamond, right sides together and aligned at the center point. Pin together, working from the T-shirt side using multiple pins. This is a bias seam, so treat the bias edges gently (no pulling!). Sew the triangle to the diamond, taking care to let your feed dogs do the work for you. Press the seams toward the triangle.

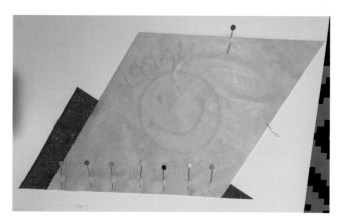

TIP

Always remember to use a pressing cloth over the motif when pressing to avoid heat on the motif. I use a piece of muslin or the back of a T-shirt.

5. Repeat Step 3 to sew a triangle to the opposite side of the diamond.

6. Repeat Step 3 for the remaining 2 corners. The block will measure approximately 15″ × 26″. Complete all blocks before trimming so you can choose an exact measurement that works for your blocks. When trimming, make sure the block has at least a ¼″ seam allowance beyond the points.

7. Depending on your layout, trim to the desired size. Our blocks were trimmed to 13½″ × 23″.

Designing the Quilt

1. Using a design wall or the floor, arrange the blocks in a pleasing design, distributing the colors to balance the quilt. Depending on the size and orientation of the finished blocks, you may need to add additional background fabric to fit them together.

2. In our quilt, we added rectangles 6½″ × 23″ of background fabric to the top and bottom of the center column. To balance the width of the quilt, we added 5½″-wide vertical sashing between each column and 6½″-wide

vertical borders. In addition to the quilt assembly diagram (below), we have included a variety of possible layouts in Alternate Quilt Ideas (page 48).

Quilt Assembly

1. Sew the rectangles together into a column. Measure each column to ensure they are the same length. If needed, add background fabric spacers as discussed in Designing the Quilt (below left).

2. Sew the 5½″ vertical sashing strips together diagonally end to end to make 2 strips 5½″ × 90½″ or the length of your columns.

3. Sew the columns together with the vertical sashing.

4. See Borders (page 15) to check your quilt measurements.

5. Sew the 6½″ outside border strips together diagonally end to end to make 2 strips 6½″ × 90½″ or the length of your quilt.

6. Sew the borders to the sides of the quilt.

7. Layer, baste, quilt, bind, and enjoy!

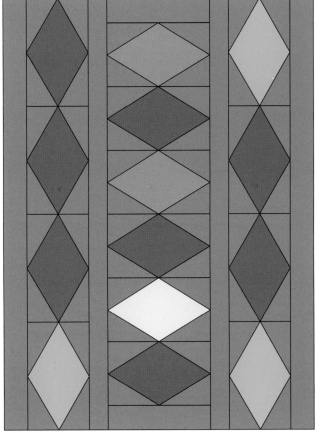

Quilt assembly

Alternate Quilt Ideas

That's My Life! variation, 25″ × 70½″. In this alternate version, the diamonds were floated on the background by trimming each block to 14½″ × 25″.

That's My Life! variation, 64½″ × 95″. In this alternate version, the diamonds were floated on the background by trimming each block to 14½″ × 25″. The top left and bottom right blocks were made up of smaller diamonds.

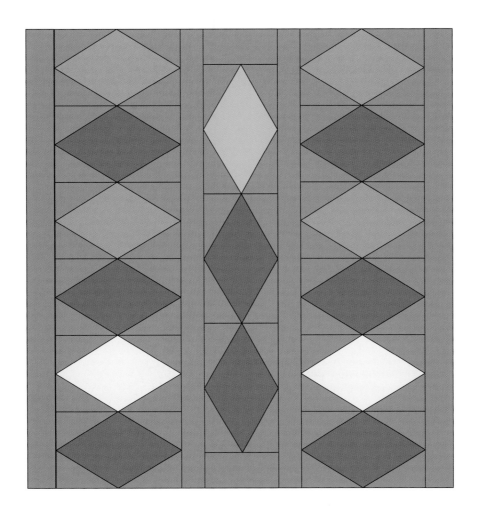

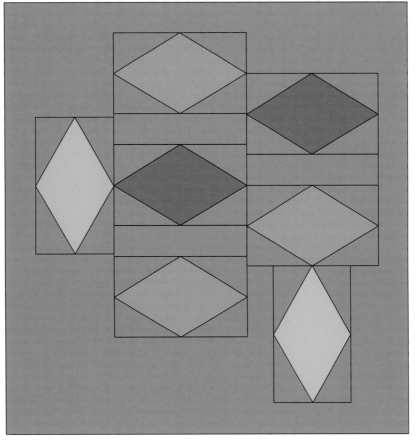

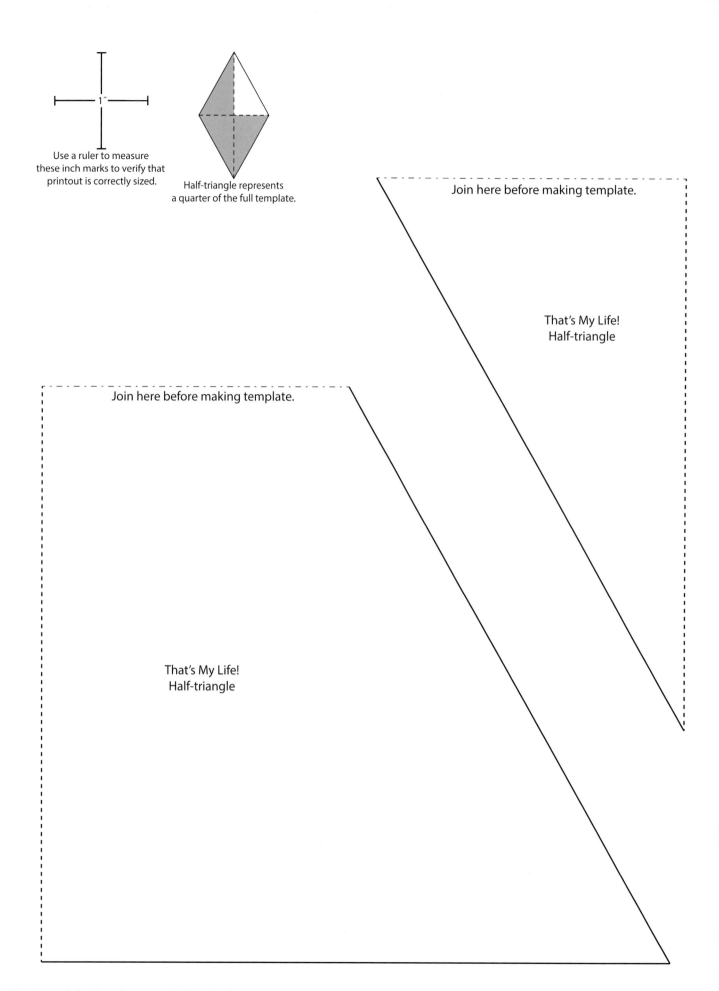

1″

Use a ruler to measure
these inch marks to verify that
printout is correctly sized.

Half-triangle represents
a quarter of the full template.

Join here before making template.

That's My Life!
Half-triangle

Join here before making template.

That's My Life!
Half-triangle

Friendship Star

Finished quilt: 58½″ × 58½″
Finished blocks: 9″ × 9″ and 13″ × 13″

Our version of *Friendship Star* allows you to use more of the clothing with fewer pieces. Some of our star points are made from parallelograms, which allows you to use a really wide motif that extends past the center of the star and into the points. To use the clothing even further, you can put motifs in the triangles that make up the remaining star points. Each star is constructed individually. There are seven large stars and sixteen small stars.

Fabric and Stabilizer

Materials are based on 40″ usable width for purchased cotton fabric.

T-shirts or clothing:

16 T-shirts with smaller motifs for small stars

7 T-shirts with larger motifs for large stars

White: 2¼ yards for star background

Stripe: 1¼ yards for corners of Star blocks (narrow stripes preferred)

Border: 1 yard

Backing: 67″ × 67″

Binding: ⅝ yard (We used the striped fabric.)

Stabilizer: 1½ yards of 60″-wide Stabili-TEE Fusible Interfacing (by C&T Publishing) or 3¼ yards of 20″-wide light- to midweight fusible interfacing, *or* Terial Magic to treat your fabric

Batting: 67″ × 67″

Template plastic: 1 sheet of 12″ × 18″

Cutting

Make a template for each of the 13″ and 9″ block parallelograms and triangles (pages 57 and 58) by tracing them onto template plastic. Trace the bold line, seam allowance line, and center point. Write "Up" on the template to easily show which side is the front. (You'll thank us later!)

T-shirts or clothing

For each star, you will need enough fabric from the same T-shirt to cut the parallelogram shape plus 2 triangles for star points. It is possible to use clothing as small as 3 months to make a small star, but be thoughtful when cutting the clothing to ensure you have enough to complete your block.

1. Prepare the clothing as explained in How to Fillet Clothing (page 7). Don't forget—if the template is larger than your T-shirt, add a portion from another section of the T-shirt to make it large enough.

2. Cut a slightly oversized parallelogram for each star— 7 large parallelograms and 16 small parallelograms.

3. Using the "Up" side of the parallelogram template, place the parallelogram template on the right side the T-shirt. The center mark on the template indicates the center of the parallelogram, which is also the center of the star.

4. Place a ruler on top of the template and use a rotary cutter to cut the parallelogram ¼″ *larger than the template.* The extra ¼″ will allow some wiggle room, since T-shirt fabric is stretchy.

Save the remaining T-shirt fabric to cut the star points in Construction (next page).

White

Large stars

Cut 3 strips 6″ × width of fabric; subcut 14 squares 6″ × 6″ for the corners.

Cut 3 strips 5¾″ × width of fabric; subcut 14 squares 5¾″ × 5¾″. Cut each in half diagonally to yield 28 triangles for the star points.

Small stars

Cut 4 strips 4¼″ × width of fabric; subcut 32 squares 4¼″ × 4¼″ for the corners.

Cut 4 strips 4″ × width of fabric; subcut 32 squares 4″ × 4″. Cut each in half diagonally to yield 64 triangles for the star points.

Stripe

Large stars

Cut 3 strips 6″ × width of fabric; subcut 14 squares 6″ × 6″ for the corners.

Small stars

Cut 4 strips 4¼″ × width of fabric; subcut 32 squares 4¼″ × 4¼″ for the corners.

Stabilizer

Use templates made from the parallelogram patterns (pages 57 and 58) to cut the parallelograms. Make sure you mark the front or "Up" side of each template. When you cut the fusible, take care to be sure that the fusible (bumpy) side of the interfacing is up as well.

Large stars

Cut 7 squares 6″ × 6″; cut each in half diagonally to yield 14 triangles.

Cut 7 parallelograms using the 13″ block parallelogram template.

Small stars

Cut 16 squares 4½″ × 4½″; cut each in half diagonally to yield 32 triangles.

Cut 16 parallelograms using the 9″ block parallelogram template.

> **TIP**
>
> To keep organized, save the pieces for the small and large stars in separate baggies. You will thank us for this later!

Borders

See Borders (page 15) and wait until you have pieced and measured your quilt top before you cut the borders. The following sizes match the project quilt.

Cut 8 strips 3½″ × width of fabric.

Binding: Cut 7 strips 2½″ × width of fabric.

Construction

All seam allowances are a scant ¼″ unless noted otherwise. See Working with T-Shirts and Clothing (page 7) and T-Shirt Quilt Basics (page 12) for more information about the techniques used in this project.

Stabilizing and Cutting the Clothing

For each star, use 1 parallelogram and 2 triangles of interfacing.

1. Fuse the parallelogram-shaped interfacing to the wrong side of the parallelogram cut from the T-shirt.

2. Place the parallelogram template, right side down, on the wrong side of the T-shirt (on the fusible). Use a ruler and rotary cutter to trim to the size of the template.

3. Fuse the 2 oversize interfacing triangles to the wrong side of the remaining filleted T-shirt. Trim each to size using the 13″ block triangle template for the large star or the 9″ block triangle template for the small star.

Star Blocks

In these steps, you will make all the parts of the Star blocks. You will then plan the quilt layout before sewing the block parts together.

Star block

Star Points

1. Pair a 9″ block T-shirt triangle with a 4″ white triangle. With the T-shirt triangle on top, join the pair along the diagonal edge to create a star point for the small blocks. Press the seam toward the background. Make 2 for each block. Use a 13″ block T-shirt triangle and a 5¾″ triangle for the large block star points.

2. Trim the small star points to 3½″ × 3½″ and the large star points to 4⅞″ × 4⅞″.

Star Centers

1. Place a 4″ white triangle on each end of a 9″ block parallelogram, matching the triangle points. Sew together to create a rectangle. Press the seams toward the white triangles. Repeat for all small stars. Use a 5¾″ white triangle with each 13″ block parallelogram to complete the large star centers.

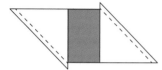 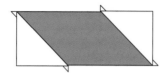

2. Trim the rectangles for the small stars to 3½″ × 9½″ and for the large stars to 4⅞″ × 13½″.

Star Corners

1. On the back of each white square 4¼″ × 4¼″ and 6″ × 6″, draw a diagonal line from the upper left corner to the lower right corner. Stack the squares with the diagonal line pointing in the same direction.

2. Separate the striped squares 4¼″ × 4¼″ into 2 piles of 16, and the striped squares 6″ × 6″ into 2 piles of 7. Make sure all stripes are oriented in the same direction and are *right side up*.

3. Turn one stack of small squares and one stack of large squares so the stripes are horizontal. Place the remaining stacks so the stripes are vertical. Keep the stacks organized!

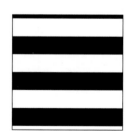 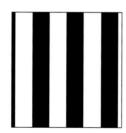

4. Place a white square with a diagonal line on top of a striped square, right sides together, and sew ¼″ on both sides of the drawn line (see Half-Square Triangles, page 14). Cut apart on the diagonal line. Press the seam toward the striped fabric.

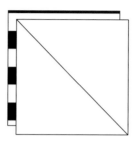 

NOTE

The striped fabric plays an important role in the design of this pattern. The stripes on the corners of the stars alternate in the layout. It is important to keep the diagonal line and the stripes in the same orientation to achieve the alternating striped pattern.

---

5. Repeat Step 4 for each white and striped pair. When sewn in the same orientation, half of your half-square triangles will have a horizontal stripe and the other half will have a vertical stripe.

6. Trim the small half-square triangles to 3½″ × 3½″ and the large stars to 4⅞″ × 4⅞″.

Plan the Layout

Before you begin assembling your blocks, decide on a layout. It's important to balance the colors of the stars so the layout is appealing. The layout will determine the direction of the stripes for the corners of each block.

TIP

It is helpful to take a picture to refer to as you assemble the quilt.

Star Block Assembly

1. Be sure the stripes are placed correctly for each star corner. The blocks in the A position must have vertically striped half-square triangles in each corner. The blocks in the B position must have horizontally striped half-square triangles in each corner.

> ### TIP
> It may be helpful to separate your blocks into an A pile and a B pile before block assembly.

2. Assemble the blocks as shown, playing close attention to the directions of the star points and the stripes.

Small stars will measure 9½″ × 9½″ square unfinished.

Large stars will measure 13½″ × 13½″ square unfinished.

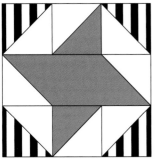

Block A

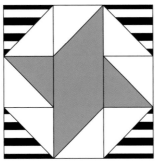

Block B

Quilt Assembly

Refer to the quilt assembly diagram (at right) and your previous block layout to keep the corner stripes in the correct orientation.

Measure your assembled quilt sections and make adjustments to the border sizes if necessary. See Borders (page 15).

1. Join the 9½″ blocks in 4 rows of 4 stars each.

Small block section assembly

2. Sew the 3½″ border strips together diagonally to make the following:

1 inner border 3½″ × 36½″

1 inner border 3½″ × 39½″

2 outer side borders 3½″ × 52½″

2 outer top and bottom borders 3½″ × 58½″

3. Sew the inner border strip 3½″ × 36½″ to the right side and press toward the border.

4. Sew the inner border strip 3½″ × 39½″ to the bottom and press toward the border.

5. Join the first 3 large stars in the bottom row. Attach the unit to the bottom of the small stars unit from Step 4. Press seams toward the inner border.

6. Join the column of 4 large Star blocks at the right side of the quilt. Attach the unit to the quilt. Press the seams toward the inner border.

7. Sew a border strip 3½″ × 52½″ to the right and left sides of the quilt. Press toward the border.

8. Sew a border strip 3½″ × 58½″ to the top and the bottom. Press toward the border.

9. Layer, baste, quilt, bind and enjoy!

Quilt assembly

Alternate Quilt Ideas

Friendship Star variation, 55″ × 68″. In this alternate version, a triple border (totaling 3″) surrounds the small blocks, and an extra row of large stars across the bottom adds to the length.

For a more formal look, try grouping the small stars in the center of the quilt. This version uses 18 small stars and 16 large stars.

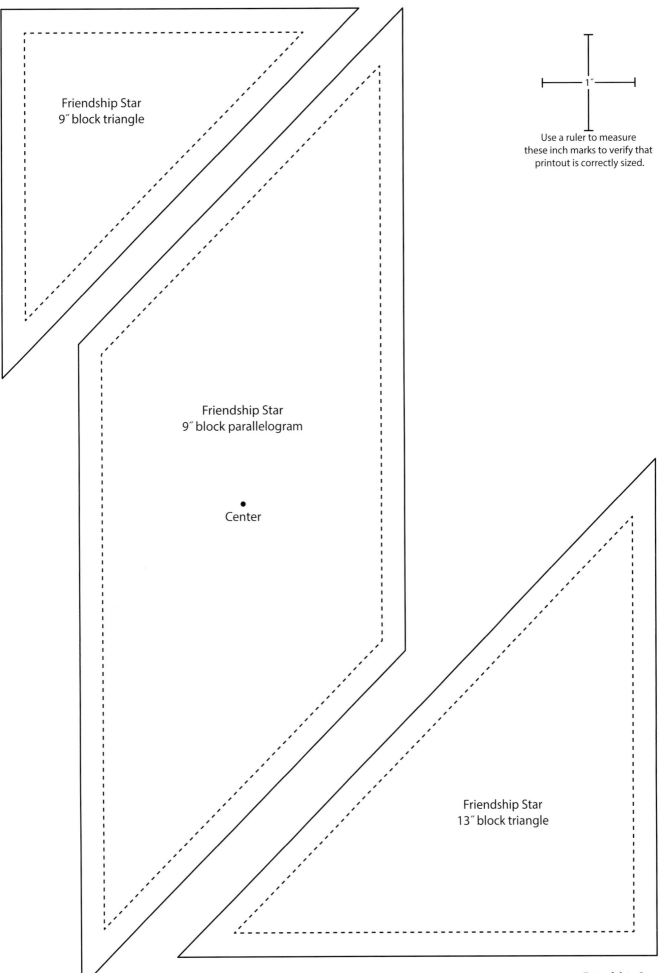

Friendship Star
9″ block triangle

Friendship Star
9″ block parallelogram

• Center

Friendship Star
13″ block triangle

1″

Use a ruler to measure
these inch marks to verify that
printout is correctly sized.

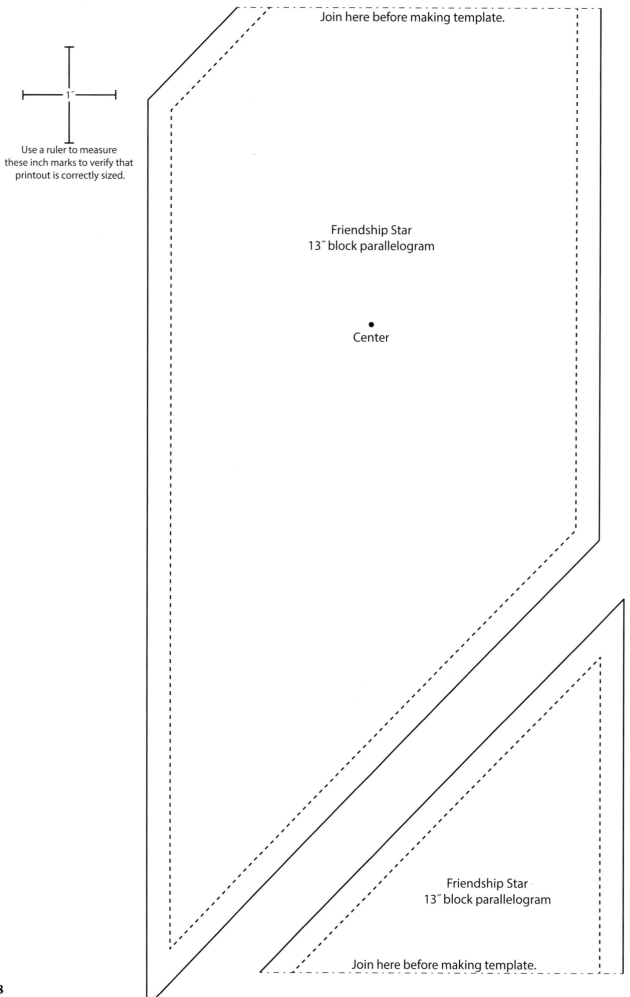

Join here before making template.

Use a ruler to measure these inch marks to verify that printout is correctly sized.

1″

Friendship Star
13″ block parallelogram

•
Center

Friendship Star
13″ block parallelogram

Join here before making template.

Always in Our Hearts

We were asked to make a T-shirt quilt for the family of a man who had passed away at a young age. It can be a challenge to design a quilt to honor someone who is no longer with us, especially since we did not know this young man.

We were very surprised when we received the bag of T-shirts. There were about 15 shirts, but someone had already cut the T-shirts apart. The shirts were red, white, black, and three shades of gray. There were no logos or motifs, just solid-colored pieces of shirts. We truly had no idea what we were going to do!

After mulling it over for a few days, we began cutting the shirts into various sizes of rectangles. We pinned the rectangles to the design wall, alternating the direction and colors to create an interesting layout. We sewed the rectangles together in blocks and then sewed the blocks together. Our client had requested that the quilt have a heart on it, so we appliquéd a red heart to the large black rectangle. The bag of T-shirt scraps had become an interesting and modern quilt, *Always in Our Hearts*.

Fabric and Stabilizer

Materials are based on 40″ usable width for purchased cotton fabric.

T-shirts: We used the scraps from 15 T-shirts and were able to cut multiple pieces from each T-shirt. If you do not have enough T-shirts, consider substituting some of the pieces with cotton fabrics.

Backing: 59″ × 79″

Binding: ⅝ yard

Stabilizer: 3½ yards of 60″-wide Stabili-TEE Fusible Interfacing (by C&T Publishing) or 10 yards of 20″-wide light- to midweight fusible interfacing, and ¼ yard of Pellon's 805 Wonder-Under or The Warm Company's Steam-A-Seam 2 for heart appliqués

Batting: 59″ × 79″

Cutting

Binding: Cut 7 strips 2½″ × width of fabric.

Stabilizer: Prior to cutting the T-shirts into the sizes in the chart (below), fillet the T-shirts and stabilize them. We stabilized the scraps and cut the fused scraps into rectangles.

T-Shirts: Set aside a 2 pieces of red T-shirt about 5″ × 10″ for the heart appliqués (page 64). If you do not have enough T-shirt material for the heart, you can use another cotton fabric in its place.

Cut the following pieces from the color indicated in the chart. Pin a scrap of paper to each rectangle to mark it with its label.

Block	Color					
	Black	**Light gray**	**Medium gray**	**Dark gray**	**Red**	**White**
1		1A: 7½″ × 3½″	1F: 5½″ × 16″	1B: 7½″ × 18″	1D: 6½″ × 3″	1C: 11½″ × 5½″ 1E: 6½″ × 13½″
2	2B: 4″ × 2½″ 2D: 4½″ × 10½″	2C: 8½″ × 3½″ 2F: 8½″ × 6″			2A: 5″ × 2½″ 2E: 4½″ × 10½″	
3	3B: 7½″ × 7½″ 3F: 9½″ × 7″ 3I: 3½″ × 7½″		3A: 14½″ × 7½″		3C: 3½″ × 7½″ 3E: 3½″ × 7″ 3J: 5½″ × 3½″	3D: 7½″ × 7″ 3G: 5½″ × 11″ 3H: 16½″ × 7½″
4	4C: 3½″ × 7½″ 4E: 3½″ × 7½″ 4F: 10½″ × 7″	4B: 10½″ × 10½″			4A: 3½″ × 7½″ 4G: 3½″ × 15″	4D: 4″ × 22″ 4H: 3½″ × 8″ 4I: 5½″ × 10½″
5	5A: 22″ × 20½″					5B: 22″ × 4½″
6	6E: 3½″ × 14″			6C: 9½″ × 7½″	6A: 5½″ × 4″	6B: 4½″ × 4″ 6D: 6½″ × 14″
7	7B: 17½″ × 3″	7A: 20″ × 4½″			7C: 3″ × 3″ 7D: 5½″ × 4″	7E: 15″ × 4″
8	8A: 10½″ × 4½″		8D: 14″ × 4½″		8C: 3½″ × 4½″	8B: 4½″ × 4½″
9	9B: 7½″ × 18½″	9A: 7½″ × 12½″ 9G: 6″ × 5″	9D: 6″ × 4½″		9E: 7½″ × 6½″ 9F: 6″ × 3½″	9C: 6″ × 7″
10	10C: 9½″ × 11½″			10D: 9½″ × 11½″	10A: 3″ × 14½″	10B: 9½″ × 3½″ 10E: 9½″ × 3½″
11	11C: 4½″ × 4″			11F: 2½″ × 8½″	11D: 3½″ × 8½″	11A: 3″ × 8½″ 11B: 4½″ × 5″ 11E: 9½″ × 8½″
12	12D: 5″ × 3½″ 12E: 10½″ × 5″				12A: 10½″ × 4½″ 12C: 6″ × 3½″	12B: 10½″ × 10½″

Construction

All seam allowances are a scant ¼″ unless noted otherwise. See Working with T-Shirts and Clothing (page 7) and T-Shirt Quilt Basics (page 12) for more information about the techniques used in this project.

Block Assembly

Sew the rectangles together in the following order, pressing the seams towards the darker fabric.

Block 1

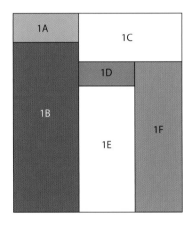

Block 2

Block 3

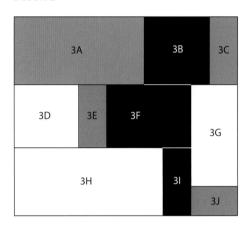

Block 1

1. Sew 1A to 1B.

2. Sew 1D to 1E.

3. Sew 1D/E to 1F.

4. Sew 1D/E/F to 1C.

5. Sew 1A/B to 1C/D/E/F.

The block measures 18½″ × 21″.

Block 2

1. Sew 2A to 2B.

2. Sew 2D to 2E.

3. Sew 2A/B to 2C.

4. Sew 2D/E to 2F.

5. Sew 2A/B/C to 2D/E/F.

The block measures 8½″ × 21″.

Block 3

1. Sew 3A to 3B.

2. Sew 3A/B to 3C.

3. Sew 3D to 3E.

4. Sew 3D/E to 3F.

5. Sew 3H to 3I.

6. Sew 3G to 3J.

7. Sew 3D/E/F to 3H/I.

8. Sew 3D/E/F/H/I to 3G/J.

9. Sew 3A/B/C to 3D/E/F/H/I/G/J

The block measures 24½″ × 21″.

Block 4

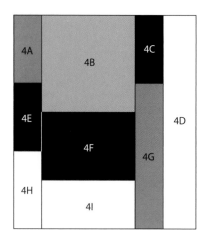

1. Sew 4A to 4E.

2. Sew 4A/E to 4H.

3. Sew 4B to 4F.

4. Sew 4B/F to 4I.

5. Sew 4C to 4G.

6. Sew 4A/E/H to 4B/F/I.

7. Sew 4C/G to 4D.

8. Sew 4A/E/H/B/F/I to 4C/G/D.

The block measures 20″ × 22½″.

Block 5

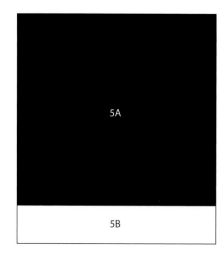

Sew 5A to 5B.

The block measures 22″ × 24½″.

Block 6

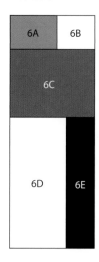

1. Sew 6A to 6B.

2. Sew 6A/B to 6C.

3. Sew 6D to 6E.

4. Sew 6A/B/C to 6D/E.

The block measures 9½″ × 24½″.

Block 7

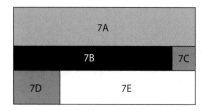

1. Sew 7B to 7C.

2. Sew 7D to 7E.

3. Sew 7A to 7B/C.

4. Sew 7A/B/C to 7D/E.

The block measures 20″ × 10½″.

Block 8

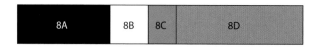

1. Sew 8A to 8B.

2. Sew 8C to 8D.

3. Sew 8A/B to 8C/D.

The block measures 31″ × 4½″.

Block 9

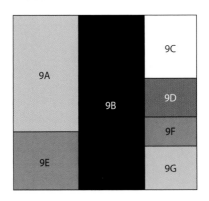

1. Sew 9A to 9E.

2. Sew 9C to 9D.

3. Sew 9F to 9G.

4. Sew 9A/E to 9B.

5. Sew 9C/D to 9F/G.

6. Sew 9A/E/B to 9C/D/F/G.

The block measures 20″ × 18½″

Block 10

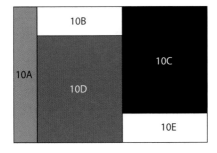

1. Sew 10B to 10D.

2. Sew 10C to 10E.

3. Sew 10A to 10B/D.

4. Sew 10A/B/D to 10C/E.

The block measures 21″ × 14½″.

Block 11

1. Sew 11B to 11C.

2. Sew 11D to 11E.

3. Sew 11A to 11B/C.

4. Sew 11D/E to 11F.

5. Sew 11A/B/C to 11D/E/F.

The block measures 21″ × 8½″.

Block 12

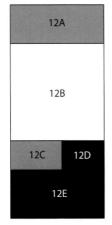

1. Sew 12A to 12B.

2. Sew 12C to 12D.

3. Sew 12C/D to 12E.

4. Sew 12A/B to 12C/D/E.

The block measures 10½″ × 22½″.

Quilt Assembly

Refer to the quilt assembly diagram (at right).

Sew the blocks together in the following order, pressing the seams toward the darker fabric.

1. Sew block 1 to block 2.

2. Sew unit 1/2 to block 3.

3. Sew block 4 to block 7.

4. Sew unit 4/7 to block 9.

5. Sew block 5 to block 6.

6. Sew unit 5/6 to block 8.

7. Sew block 10 to block 11.

8. Sew unit 10/11 to block 12.

9. Sew unit 5/6/8 to unit 10/11/12.

10. Sew unit 4/7/9 to unit 5/6/8/10/11/12.

11. Sew unit 1/2/3 to unit 4/7/9/5/6/8/10/11/12.

Quilt assembly

Adding the Heart

The heart patterns are in reverse. They are ready to trace on the fusible web so that the heart will be in the correct orientation once pressed to the red T-shirt or fabric.

1. Trace the templates onto fusible web.

2. Fuse to the red T-shirt or fabric.

3. Cut the shapes from the fabric.

4. Fuse in place in the center of block 5, referring to the photo (page 59).

5. Layer, baste, quilt, bind, and enjoy!

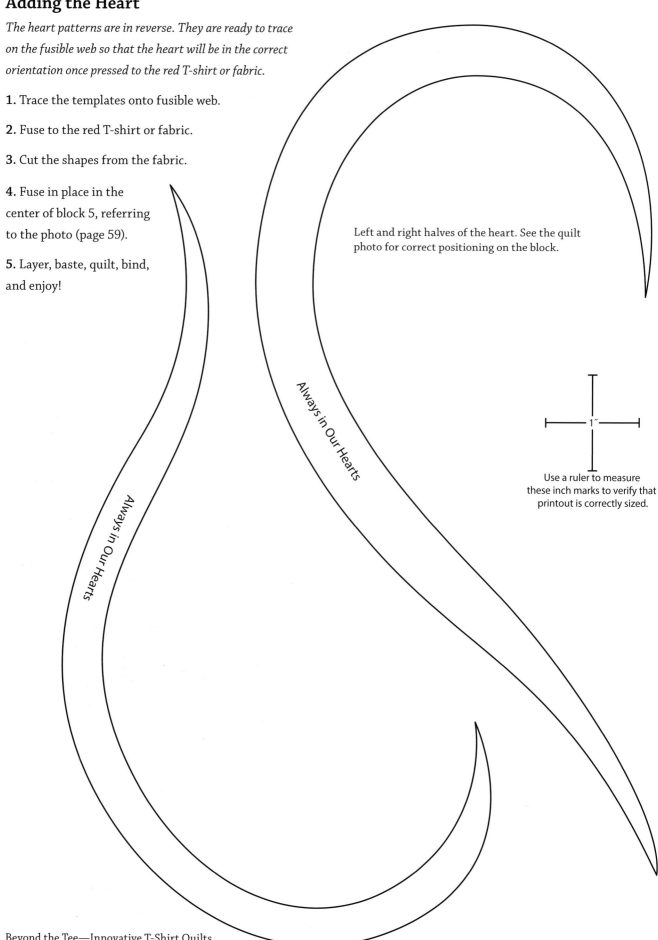

Left and right halves of the heart. See the quilt photo for correct positioning on the block.

Always in Our Hearts

Always in Our Hearts

Always in Our Hearts

1″

Use a ruler to measure these inch marks to verify that printout is correctly sized.

Stars 1-2-3

Finished quilt: 52½″ × 72½″
Finished blocks: 4″ × 4″, 8″ × 8″, and 12″ × 12″

Our first *Stars 1-2-3* was a baby quilt, but we liked it so much that we made this one bigger and used clothing to complete our stars. It is a great pattern with or without the clothing. Our original was in scrappy turquoise fabrics and remains one of our favorite designs.

This pattern requires that each star be constructed individually. There are 11 large stars, 22 medium stars, and 24 small stars. If you wish, you can replace some of the small stars with background squares.

Fabric and Stabilizer

Materials are based on 40˝ usable width for purchased cotton fabric.

Clothing: We used around 20 pieces of clothing for the stars. The fabrics from the little girl's colorful dresses were used several times, which helps move the eye around the quilt. These dresses were toddler size with full skirts, which gave us quite a bit of fabric. See the cutting directions for the pieces you will need for each star.

If you don't have quite enough fabric for all of the stars, consider making a few stars from complementary cotton fabrics.

White (or your choice): 3 yards for background

Backing: 61˝ × 81˝

Binding: ⅝ yard

Stabilizer: 2 yards of 60˝-wide Stabili-TEE Fusible Interfacing (by C&T Publishing) or 5 yards of 20˝-wide light- to midweight fusible interfacing, *or* Terial Magic to treat your fabric

Batting: 61˝ × 81˝

> **NOTE**
> This yardage assumes stabilizer is needed for all T-shirts or clothing in the quilt. If it's not a stretchy fabric—like a T-shirt or knit—you do not need to use stabilizer.

Cutting

Clothing: Prepare the clothing as explained in How to Fillet Clothing (page 7). See Construction (next page) for cutting instructions.

> **NOTE**
> Each star requires 1 center square and 8 half-square triangles.

White

Large stars

Cut 5 strips 4˝ × width of fabric; subcut 44 squares 4˝ × 4˝ for the star-point backgrounds.

Cut 4 strips 3½˝ × width of fabric; subcut 44 squares 3½˝ × 3½˝ for the Star block corners.

Medium stars

Cut 7 strips 3˝ × width of fabric; subcut 88 squares 3˝ × 3˝ for the star-point backgrounds.

Cut 6 strips 2½˝ × width of fabric; subcut 88 squares 2½˝ × 2½˝ for the Star block corners.

Small stars

Cut 5 strips 2˝ × width of fabric; subcut 96 squares 2˝ × 2˝ for the star-point backgrounds.

Cut 4 strips 1½˝ × width of fabric; subcut 96 squares 1½˝ × 1½˝ for the Star block corners.

Background fill-in blocks

Cut 3 strips 4½˝ × width of fabric; subcut 23 squares 4½˝ × 4½˝.

Binding

Cut 7 strips 2½˝ × width of fabric

Stabilizer

Large stars

Cut 11 squares 7˝ × 7˝.

Cut 44 squares 4˝ × 4˝.

Medium stars

Cut 22 squares 5˝ × 5˝.

Cut 88 squares 3˝ × 3˝

Small stars

Cut 24 squares 3˝ × 3˝.

Cut 96 squares 2˝ × 2˝.

> **TIP**
> There are many pieces in this quilt. To keep organized, put the interfacing pieces in small baggies or envelopes with a notation such as "7˝ fusible squares for the large stars." Repeat for the background fabric and the T-shirts. Once you have fused the interfacing to the T-shirt fabric and trimmed to size, save the pieces in baggies with a notation such as "Large stars: star points." You will thank us for this later!

Construction

All seam allowances are a scant ¼″ unless noted otherwise. See Working with T-Shirts and Clothing (page 7) and T-Shirt Quilt Basics (page 12) for more information about the techniques used in this project.

Stabilizing and Cutting the Clothing

If the interfacing becomes distorted while you are fusing the star point squares to the clothing, don't worry. Go ahead and trim the fused square to size, centering the fused interfacing.

Large stars

1. Fuse 1 interfacing square 7″ × 7″ and 4 interfacing squares 4″ × 4″ to the knit clothing.

2. Cut the following:

• 1 square 6½″ × 6½″ for the star center

• 4 squares 4″ × 4″ for the star points

3. Repeat Steps 1 and 2 to prepare 11 large stars.

Medium Stars

1. Fuse 1 interfacing square 5″ × 5″ and 4 interfacing squares 3″ × 3″ to the knit clothing.

2. Cut the following:

• 1 square 4½″ × 4½″ for the star center

• 4 squares 3″ × 3″ for the star points

3. Repeat Steps 1 and 2 to prepare 22 medium stars.

Small Stars

1. Fuse 1 interfacing square 3″ × 3″ and 4 interfacing squares 2″ × 2″ to the knit clothing.

2. Cut the following:

• 1 square 2½″ × 2½″ for the star center

• 4 squares 2″ × 2″ for the star points

3. Repeat Steps 1 and 2 to prepare 24 small stars.

Star Point Assembly

1. Refer to Half-Square Triangles (page 14) and use the star-point background squares and the fused star-point clothing squares to make the following half-square triangles:

• 88 large half-square triangles measuring 3½″ × 3½″

• 176 medium half-square triangles measuring 2½″ × 2½″

• 192 small half-square triangles measuring 1½″ × 1½″

2. Sew the half-square triangles together in pairs to make the star points as shown in the Star block assembly diagram (below). You will need 44 large, 88 medium, and 96 small star points.

Block Assembly

Using 4 background squares, 4 star points, and 1 center square, assemble each star following the diagram below.

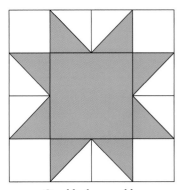

Star block assembly

Quilt Assembly

1. We encourage you to lay out your quilt on a design wall, the floor, or even a bed to help to distribute the color throughout. Refer to the quilt assembly diagram (next page).

2. Assemble the blocks and filler background squares into the following units.

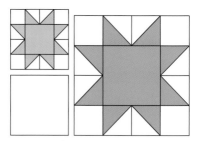

Unit 1: Make 6.

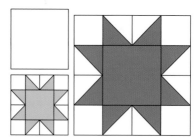

Unit 2: Make 4.

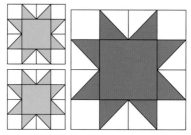

Unit 3: Make 1.

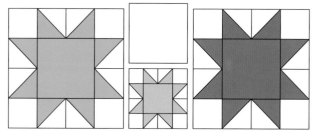

Unit 4: Make 4.

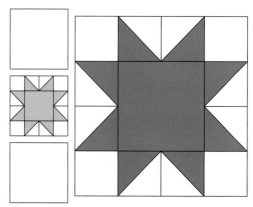

Unit 5: Make 2.

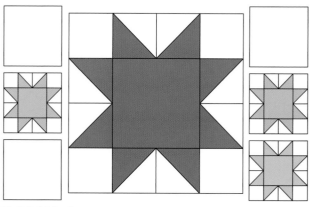

Unit 6: Make 1.

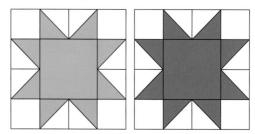

Unit 7: Make 1.

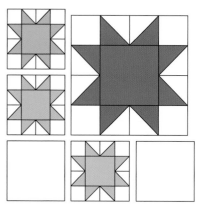

Unit 8: Make 1.

Quilt assembly

3. Referring to the quilt assembly diagram, add the remaining 12˝ blocks to the units.

4. Sew the units into rows.

5. Sew the rows together.

6. Layer, baste, quilt, bind, and enjoy!

Alternate Quilt Ideas

A. Alternate layout of *Stars 1-2-3* using turquoise fabrics 40˝ × 48˝. This version has 6 large, 11 medium, and 22 small stars.

B. Alternate colorway of *Stars 1-2-3* using red, white, and blue

Special Concepts

In this chapter, we will show you some special ideas for making quilts from clothing. We provide you with an idea, rather than a pattern, to create your T-shirt quilt.

Finding a consistent theme: *Delaney's Travels* (next page)

Tie quilts—why not? (page 72)

Memories from scraps: *The Mom Quilt* (page 77)

The Mom Pillow (page 77)

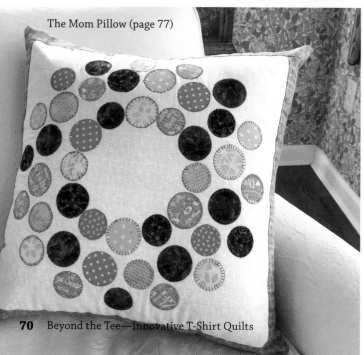

Finding a Consistent Theme:
Delaney's Travels

Delaney's Travels, 74˝ × 85˝

Delaney's Travels was a collaborative effort with our client. Delaney's mom, Dana, brought us a collection of Delaney's T-shirts from toddler through high school. The family travelled extensively and many of the shirts came from far and wide.

The Process

Dana had an idea of how she wanted the quilt to look. When we sat down to discuss her thoughts, we sketched a rough draft of a possible layout.

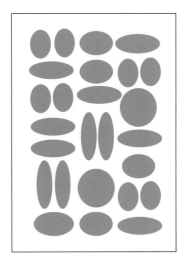

Since the shapes are all similar in nature, we began by cutting ovals from nonfusible stabilizer to determine what size oval was needed for each motif. We traced platters from the kitchen and printed shapes from word-processing and presentation programs to get our ovals; then we fine-tuned the sizes of the ovals based on the motifs we had. We ended up with nine oval shapes—some long and narrow, others wider and more circular—to accommodate each T-shirt. We then sorted the T-shirts by oval size. Once we identified the appropriate oval for each motif, we traced the oval for each T-shirt onto nonfusible stabilizer.

> ### TIP
> There are free templates available on the internet. Search for "oval template" or whatever shape inspires you.

Next, we prepared our T-shirts following the instructions in How to Fillet Clothing (page 7) and Choosing a Stabilizer (page 12). Once they were stabilized, we matched the ovals traced on nonfusible stabilizer with each motif.

With the T-shirt right side up, we centered the nonfusible stabilizer oval on each motif and pinned. We stitched around each oval, cut a slit in the stabilizer, and turned the oval right side out, following the same process used in *Circle Gets the Square!*, Construct the Circles (page 33).

Next, we pinned our background to the design wall and began designing. Dana liked the idea of having the oval shapes float on a background fabric, rather than placing each oval into a square or rectangular block, as we did in *Circle Gets the Square!*. We used a colorful polka dot fabric in Delaney's favorite color for the background.

We randomly pinned a number of the ovals on the background and then moved them around. We balanced the size, direction, and color of the motifs to create a cohesive look.

You have to start somewhere—just get it up on the wall!

We discovered that some of the T-shirts just didn't look right on the background. We set them aside and added them to the back of the quilt.

Once we decided on the layout, we pinned each motif to background and took the quilt off the design wall.

Since this quilt was rather large, it was a bit awkward to work with. Basting each motif was imperative for keeping them in place. Using a long stitch, we hand basted each motif to the background and removed the pins. This step may also be completed on a domestic or longarm sewing machine. We also could have used Roxanne Glue-Baste-It to secure each motif to the background.

Using the buttonhole stitch on the sewing machine, we stitched each motif to the background, varying the thread color and stitch size for the different motifs.

Once all the motifs were attached to the background, we layered, quilted, and bound the quilt.

Tie Quilts—Why Not?

Happy Retirement, Mr. Smith, 20˝ × 20˝

With a little patience and preparation, you can make neckties a great way to incorporate clothing into a quilt. The scale of the print on the ties is unique in that it makes a big statement in a small area.

We tend to use ties more in wallhangings than large quilts, often because a bag of ties doesn't go as far as a bin of T-shirts! Ties can be used in quilts that are traditional or modern, elaborate or simple, sophisticated or playful. Most ties are well made and can be successfully used in quilts.

Prepping Ties

1. To determine whether a tie will stand up to the construction of the quilt, begin by simply throwing the ties in the washing machine on a regular cycle with a mild detergent.

> **TIP**
>
> Put them in a lingerie bag to avoid a knotted mess at the end of the cycle.

2. Hang them to dry; then inspect them to see if the fabric has remained intact without shredding or falling apart. They don't need to look pristine or as if they could be worn again; the fibers must simply remain intact.

3. If there is a label on the back of the tie, remove it and set it aside. Labels sometimes make a great embellishment to tie quilts. Or you can make a label with the labels (see Creating Labels, page 16, for more information).

Remove Stitches

1. From the back of the tie's narrow end, snip approximately 2″ of the stitching holding the tie closed.

2. Once you remove the first few inches of stitches, you'll sometimes notice that the tie is held together by a chain stitch that is easily removed by lightly tugging on the thread.

3. Pull the thread; the entire tie will become unsewn. If the tie is not sewn together with a chain stitch, continue removing the stitches using small scissors or snips.

Pulling the chain-stitched seam

4. Open the tie, discard the interlining, and trim away the lining at either end.

> **TIP**
>
> Are you surprised at how much fabric you have to work with? The fabric is usually more than 50″ long and varies in width from around 4½″ at the narrow end to around 8½″ at the wide end.

Attaching Interfacing

When using ties, we recommend a nonwoven medium-weight fusible interfacing. Tie fabric is cut on the bias, so treat it with care to keep it from distorting or stretching.

1. Carefully place the tie, wrong side up, on your ironing surface.

2. To maintain the pattern design on the tie, gently pat it into shape and press, using a pressing cloth and a medium-hot iron.

3. Depending on the size of the pieces required for your project, cut the interfacing to the appropriate size and fuse to the back of the tie.

> **NOTE**
> We usually put interfacing on the entire tie. That way, our leftover ties are ready to use as fabric in our next project.

Paper Piecing

Due to size and scale of the prints on the ties, we often find that our tie projects benefit from foundation or paper piecing. This is not a rule, however. We have created many successful projects using these and other techniques.

The design possibilities are endless with paper piecing. A wonderful website called Wombat Quilts (wombatquilts.com) offers fabulous *free* paper-piecing patterns. We used their pattern Icky Thump to create the quilt *Kicking and Screaming* (someone didn't want to give up his ties, but he loves the quilt). The outer border was also paper pieced using traditional Diamond-in-a-Rectangle and Square-in-a-Square blocks.

Kicking and Screaming, 27˝ × 27˝

Foundation Piecing

We constructed *Happy Retirement, Mr. Smith* using the flip-and-sew method with aspects of paper piecing thrown in. It has a nonfusible foundation to maintain consistency in the spacing of each tie block.

Happy Retirement, Mr. Smith, 20˝ × 20˝

Detail of *Happy Retirement, Mr. Smith*

Mr. Smith, an elementary school teacher, wore fun ties given to him by his students. We wanted to represent his years of teaching and the ties in a format that would suggest a filmstrip depicting snapshots of his daily life.

In this quilt, the tie blocks were 3˝ × 3˝ square, fussy cut to center the motifs. The vertical sashing is cut ¾˝ wide × 4˝ long. Our tie blocks finished at 2½˝ × 2½˝ with the vertical sashing at ¼˝ and the horizontal sashing at 1˝.

We used nonfusible stabilizer as the foundation (see Choosing a Stabilizer, page 12). For each row, we cut a strip of the foundation 4˝ wide. Leaving about 2˝ at the beginning of the strip, we drew lines across the strip, 2½˝ for the finished size of the tie block and ¼˝ for the vertical sashing, and repeated for the number of blocks we needed. If the size of your tie block is larger or smaller than 3˝, you will need to adjust the size of the strip.

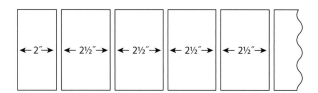

We placed the rows on an angle so the length of each row varied. As you decide on your layout, determine whether your rows will be on an angle or in a traditional horizontal row. Depending on your layout, the number of blocks in each row may vary.

We placed the first motif faceup about 2˝ from the end of the foundation strip. (The 2˝ of open space at the beginning of the strip gives you space to add sashing to the left of the motif, if necessary, and offers flexibility to add a portion of a motif, if desired.) Pin a strip of sashing (the sashing extends above and below the lines) to the right side of the motif, right sides together. Turn over the foundation and sew through all 3 layers using the first vertical line as your sewing line.

Flip the sashing away from the tie and press, using a pressing cloth. Trim as you would trim a paper-pieced block by using an Add-a-Quarter ruler and card stock to keep the accurate placement of the tie squares. Add the next motif to the sashing and repeat the process to complete the row. Your layout determines the number of rows needed.

We cut the horizontal sashing 1½˝ wide and fused a small piece of fabric with wonky lines of circles to each sashing to give the illusion of a filmstrip.

Traditional Quilt Designs

Our *Roman Coins* tie sampler is a traditional variation of the retirement quilt. The blocks are rectangular, and the layout is more organized, but we used the same foundation-piecing process to create it.

Roman Coins, 14″ × 16″

Tie Labels

Those labels from the backs of ties? Try using them to create a custom label for your quilt.

Memories from Scraps: *The Mom Quilt*

The Mom Quilt, 33″ × 33″

The Mom Pillow, 18″ × 18″

We are often asked to make clothing quilts by moms with more than one child. These moms often plan to put away the quilts until their children are old enough to appreciate them. What a wonderful gift for a graduation or first apartment!

What the moms often forget is they are the ones who best remember their kids in these clothes. And just like moms do, they give this wonderful gift back to their children. We decided to make just a little something for mom each time we make quilts for her children.

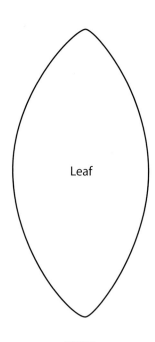

Leaf

1¾″ circle

1½″ circle

The Process

1. When we cut up the clothing, we end up with scraps of many colors and sizes. All of the scraps get thrown into a bucket, just in case we need a small piece to complete a quilt. Once the quilts are finished, we use the scraps to make a wallhanging or pillow for mom to keep.

2. We have provided patterns for a few different shapes (at left). Trace the shape multiple times onto fusible web (such as Wonder-Under or Steam-a-Seam 2); then fuse to the back of your scraps.

3. Cut out the shapes and arrange on a background fabric in a pleasing layout. Use our ideas or your imagination to come up with your own unique design.

4. Fuse the shapes to the background fabric.

5. Quilt as desired.

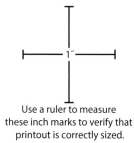

1″

Use a ruler to measure these inch marks to verify that printout is correctly sized.

About the Authors

Mary Cannizzaro and **Jen Cannizzaro** are mother and daughter, friends, and business partners. They are two of the most energetic people you will ever meet.

Mary remembers the sewing machine on the dining room table of her childhood home, moved only on Sundays to make room for the family's dinner. Mary learned how to sew at an early age and began quilting in the early 1990s, when her hometown asked for volunteers to make blocks for a raffle quilt. She is an award-winning quilter who has shown her quilts in international shows.

Jen is a software trainer by day, quilter by night and weekend. Quilting fell into her lap accidentally in the early 2000s, when she took the place of one of Mary's friends who was unable to attend classes she had signed up for. Her first quilt, *Self-Portrait of Jen as a Redhead*, finished at 7″ square and became their company logo years later.

In 2014, the duo opened Cannizzaro Creations, a quilting studio in Rockland, Massachusetts. They began longarm quilting for many quilters in the area, with Mary traveling to Massachusetts a few times a month to quilt. They have been commissioned to create dozens of quilts for fans of their work.

Visit Mary and Jen online and follow on social media!

Website: canquilt.com

Facebook: /canquilt

Instagram: @cannizzarocreations

Photo by Matthew Burstein

Mary Cannizzaro (*left*) and Jen Cannizzaro (*right*)

Self-Portrait of Jen as a Redhead, 7″ × 7″, by Jen Cannizzaro, 2002

Jen's first quilt. Mary hoped her children would have her red hair, but it wasn't meant to be, so Jen made her self-portrait with red hair. It's been our logo from the beginning of our partnership.